LIGHT Y
SALES

FOR EXPLOSIVE CUSTOMER GROWTH

REESE GOMEZ

We help busy professionals write and publish their stories
to distinguish themselves and their brands.

(407) 287-5700 | Winter Park, FL
info@BrightRay.com | www.BrightRay.com

ISBN: 978-1-956464-39-9

Published in the United States of America.

PRAISE FOR LIGHT YOUR SALES FUSE

"A must-read for healthcare software, services, and technology leaders. Reese shows how to scale it! I've personally experienced the power and results of the approach. Now this book scales access to all by laying out the step-by-step process with real examples and metrics."

SCOTT WHYTE,
PARTNER, HEALTH ENTERPRISE PARTNERS

"The SalesSparx FUSE process is a primary ingredient in the growth strategy of our portfolio companies. Reese and his team have proven to us that the process works, and we work with him and his team frequently."

DAVE VREELAND,
SENIOR MANAGING PARTNER,
CADUCEUS CAPITAL PARTNERS

"The SalesSparx FUSE process has become the connective tissue of our company in terms of how we execute and communicate our customer relationships. Larger deal sizes, better conversion rates, and shorter sales cycles are the result."

DEAN FREDENBURGH,
CRO, CLEARDATA

"The FUSE insights and methods really work. I have had the pleasure of assisting Reese and his team on several projects that resulted in tremendous company growth."

RUSS RUDISH,
FORMER GLOBAL HEALTHCARE LEADER, DELOITTE

"I have seen great healthcare products or services not achieve their sales potential. SalesSparx FUSE is filled with insights that cover both the science and the art of achieving rapid growth."

MITCHELL MORRIS, MD,
FORMER VICE CHAIR AND GLOBAL LEADER OF LIFE SCIENCES AND HEALTHCARE, DELOITTE

"SalesSparx FUSE is an instant MBA on how to scale and grow your B2B business. Having personally partnered with hundreds of companies on their go-to-market efforts, I can confirm that Reese Gomez delivers proven insights coupled with the practical details you need on how to transform your business and drive accelerating success."

MARK CORLEY,
COO, JUMPCREW

"This book is a must-have resource for any company looking for a proven, systematic approach to sell game-changing solutions in healthcare."

ANTHONY MCCARLEY,
CEO, MCCARLEY INTERNATIONAL

"Reese and team were invaluable to me as a fledgling sales VP tasked with aggressive revenue targets while pivoting to a consultative sales model. Thanks to SalesSparx, we exceeded our revenue targets and increased average deal size by three times, ultimately leading to an acquisition by a strategic buyer for a much higher valuation."

JOHN EVANS,
VP OF DIGITAL OPERATIONS,
EVERGREEN HEALTHCARE PARTNERS

"FUSE offers a pioneering step-by-step approach that is pragmatic and easy to follow to connect to our healthcare providers!"

ARVIND KUMAR,
DIGITAL HEALTH LEADER, EISNERAMPER,
FORMER PARTNER, PWC

"I can enthusiastically say that the SalesSparx FUSE collaborative process dramatically helped our healthcare technology company transform from a traditional software sales approach to one that, as Reese emphasizes, "moves from selling to buyers to selling with them." This focus change reshaped our sales approach and increased our sales results by 10 times."

JEFF ARONSON,
PRESIDENT, EQUIPX

Thanks Mom and Dad

for your unconditional love

TABLE OF CONTENTS

CHAPTER THREE
Offering Maturity

CHAPTER FOUR
Marketing Maturity

CHAPTER FIVE
Sales Maturity—Culture, Model, and Process

CHAPTER SIX
Sales Maturity—The Revenue Machine

CHAPTER SEVEN
Delivery Maturity

CHAPTER EIGHT
Enablement Technology Maturity

AUTHOR'S NOTE

First, congratulations on achieving success in building a business-to-business (B2B) company. To reach this point, you and your team have done a great job selling change in process, technology, and user behavior. Complex sales require creativity, flexibility, and collaboration. You "nailed it," so now how do you scale sales faster? Many companies have great offerings but do not achieve their full growth potential without a proven go-to-market playbook. The SalesSparx FUSE process fixes this problem. While FUSE can work for any company that sells complex solutions, the case studies and examples in this book are dedicated to healthcare. The healthcare industry in the United States and across the globe is at a major inflection point, and the status quo is likely unsustainable. Helping high-potential companies drive innovation in the market is part of the long-term solution. Since founding SalesSparx in 2014, my partners and I have had the honor of working with amazing investors, CEOs, and sales and marketing leaders across 100+ healthcare companies to improve go-to-market maturity and, as a result, accelerate innovation and sales. In the most successful companies, the CEO—or for larger companies, the head of the business unit—"owns" the go-to-market strategy, and sales, marketing, and other key company leaders and their teams provide input and execute. I hope that the FUSE process, insights, and real-world stories herein will help your company on its journey with your customers to make healthcare better.

INTRODUCTION

I was about to graduate from Stanford University as an industrial engineer when a prominent healthcare company invited me to interview for a job. After the conversation, I could see great potential in the role. Realizing the importance of my decision, I talked to my professor and advisor. She gave an answer I wasn't expecting: "Don't go into healthcare. You can't control variance."

All industrial engineering students learn one core lesson: repeatability is the key to a quality result. A medication can cure one person but elicit an allergic reaction in another. People can have identical diagnoses but, due to genetics, experience different outcomes from the same treatment protocol. Doctors are trained in different schools with different areas of focus and depth of expertise, and health systems are constructed to support diverse patient needs. There are thousands of health plans and reimbursement models in various countries and markets. As a result, each healthcare organization that we work with—whether it be a health system, physician practice, life sciences organization, or medical device company—significantly differs from its peers. Because of this variance, the change in process, technology, and user behavior are much harder to understand and manage. Marketing and selling healthcare software, business services, or other technology requires more iteration and collaboration between a buyer and seller to define problems, design solutions, and manage the change. This complexity exists whether the focus is to decrease costs, improve quality and safety, reduce provider burnout, enhance patient experience, or increase revenue profitability.

FROM NAILING IT TO SCALING IT

Working in management consulting firms and software companies, my team and I recognized a vital knowledge gap as companies moved from nailing their offering, i.e. finding product-market fit, to scaling sales. Figure I.1 below shows the gap between the phases.

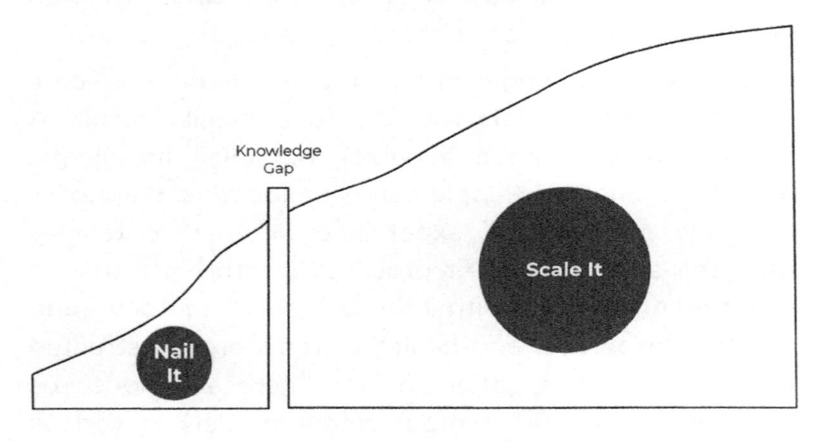

Figure I.1

(See page 143)

This knowledge gap deprives potentially great companies of growing and hinders the pace of innovation in the market. A surplus of methodologies exists for business strategy, company culture, and product-market fit, but almost no industry-specific information is readily available for scaling sales past those initial phases. Post the "nail it" phase, offerings will unpredictably hit or miss. Alternatively, some companies will try to scale too early, which leads to over-promising and under-delivering. You can't build a business one ticked-off customer at a time.

As the healthcare-focused B2B organizations my team and I worked with encountered these sales growth challenges, there appeared to be no widely available model to guide go-to-market maturation. A one-size-fits-all approach did not work. The companies needed a standardized yet versatile approach that could address their individual problems. Amid the complex sales scaling process, there laid a window of opportunity to create an iterative action plan for reaching—and in many cases, exceeding—rapid growth objectives.

SALESSPARX FUSE™ IDEATION AND DEVELOPMENT

In 2014, my partners and I established SalesSparx, a now international sales acceleration company that enables high-potential businesses to sell more, faster. At that point in my career, I had begun formulating a playbook for helping healthcare B2B organizations transform their market potential into market share, but I had yet to put it to paper. I had just completed a three-year effort during which I led the management consulting division of a healthcare IT professional services firm from $0 to $60 million in revenue while the overall company grew from $50 million to $250 million over the same period. We had a great team, won Best in KLAS for overall professional services, and ranked number one or two in almost every service area we competed in. We were also named the top place to work in our category.

I was part of the three-person team, including our CFO and CEO, who worked with our investment bankers to develop and deliver the pitch to sell the company for what was then a record valuation. Prior to this experience, I had also led or been part of the leadership team in multiple other companies where we achieved more than 50–100 percent year-over-year growth. Along the way, I learned from these experiences and some very smart people, but for the most part, we operated with "unconscious competence." I always wondered what we could have accomplished with a proven playbook to follow.

My partners and I took our decades-long industry experience and spent nearly two years and more than 10,000 hours researching best practices for a simple yet comprehensive model to drive sales and revenue growth. We spent a substantial amount of time researching B2B sales and marketing best practices, but we garnered our most valuable insights from our experience and first-hand interviews with healthcare industry leaders and executives. I knew many of these experts from my alma mater and business network, which included leaders of transformative software companies, partners at major management consulting firms, and other business pioneers. The graphic in Figure I.2 below highlights some of our key findings.

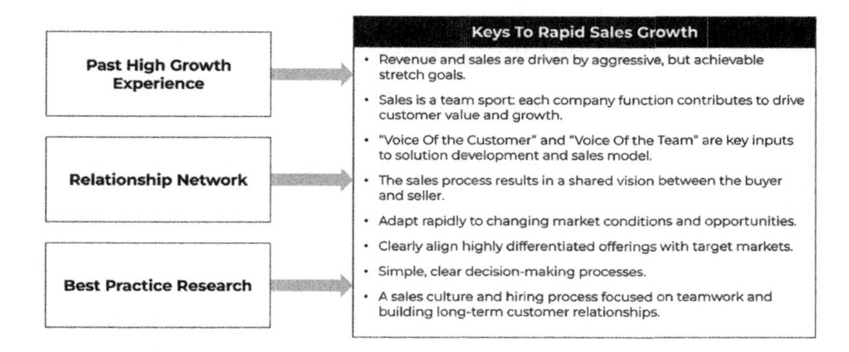

Figure I.2
(See page 144)

The result of these insights is the SalesSparx FUSE™. FUSE is a continuous process to iteratively accelerate go-to-market (GTM) maturity. Once you light the FUSE, your company will achieve the higher levels of maturity required to sell more, faster.

HOW TO USE THIS BOOK

The first step we recommend is to carefully read Chapter One, which outlines the entire FUSE process. After that, Chapters 2–8 provide detail on each FUSE GTM maturity component and guidance on how to assess where you are today and what you need to do to advance to the next level. Each chapter begins with a summary of key takeaways and ends with sample GTM maturity assessment criteria and a SalesSparx case study. Finally, once you have learned about the GTM components, you will reach the FUSE Implementation Playbook. The playbook will provide a step-by-step action plan to ignite the FUSE for your organization.

There are countless books that outline how to understand what business you are in, your overall business strategy, and how to find product-market fit.[1] This book builds upon that fundamental knowledge, detailing how to design the go-to-market component of your business strategy by assessing each of the GTM components on a continuum that starts with Emerging, moves to Basic, then Advanced, and finally Leading. As your company moves to higher levels of maturity in each component, you will more rapidly scale sales. FUSE assumes you have already developed some capability in each area and will help you understand the gaps that will impede future rapid growth. As you can see in Figure I.3 below, by using FUSE, you can iteratively move from your current level of GTM maturity in each GTM component to an accelerated future state.

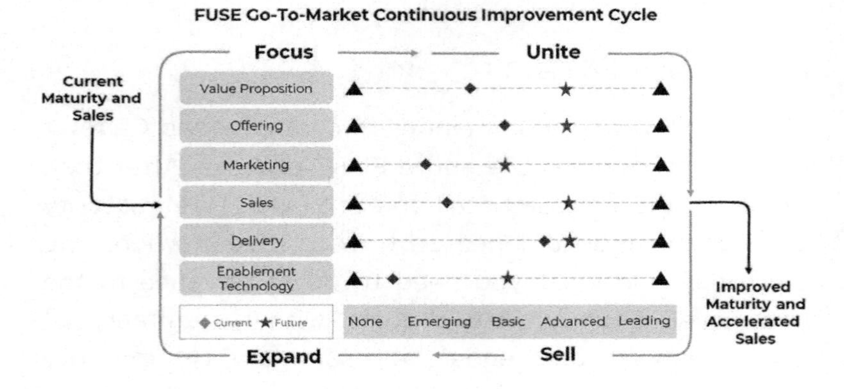

Figure I.3
(See page 145)

Because FUSE is built for companies that have already achieved strong evidence of product-market fit and are looking to scale faster, startups may not find optimal value in this book's content. In contrast, small-to-medium-sized healthcare companies or a newer healthcare division of a large company can be FUSE-enabled to achieve rapid growth targets. SalesSparx primarily partners with companies that have a viable business strategy but want to grow faster. It is critical that the business and GTM strategy are clearly aligned and evolve together in a unified way.

My hope is that, after reading this book, you will envision the roadmap to scaling sales successfully. By the last chapter, you should have concrete answers to the "Three Whys" for your buyers:

- Why do they need to change?
- Why now?
- Why is your company the right choice to help with the change?

I've seen many companies with transformative ideas fail before reaching a point where they can scale, and I've seen many beneficial innovations become lost in the process. This book aims to supply you with tools, resources, and a mindset for expediting progress. SalesSparx dedicates itself to making a holistic difference in healthcare, but our company cannot reach every customer or every company. By writing a comprehensive guide, we aim to make our knowledge readily available so that organizations can increase the probability of their success andB push needed healthcare innovations into the market. Then, as you begin answering the Three Whys, not only will your answers evolve, but your company will evolve alongside them.

CHAPTER ONE

The FUSE Process

CHAPTER SUMMARY

- **SalesSparx FUSE (Focus, Unite, Sell, Expand)** is an iterative process to accelerate go-to-market maturity, resulting in faster sales growth. It can be applied to any B2B company whose offerings require a moderate to significant change in process, technology, and end-user behavior and is especially appropriate for selling into the healthcare space.
- **Focus:** Companies establish a stretch goal, which has two components: a very aggressive but achievable sales target and a "make healthcare better" target.
- **Unite:** With a clear target, an organization's leaders and teams work toward that goal and create a go-to-market (GTM) plan to achieve it.
- **Sell:** The GTM plan enables the sales teams to improve the offering by collecting customer feedback and advancing each component of the GTM plan.
- **Expand:** Companies can build upon their experiences by incorporating feedback, adjusting the business to achieve better results, and scaling by using replicable processes. The process continuously repeats to scale sales performance.

SalesSparx FUSE is an iterative, continuous process to improve go-to-market (GTM) maturity. While FUSE is appropriate for any company selling complex offerings in complex environments, it is especially appropriate for healthcare software, technology, and professional services companies. It facilitates assessing maturity, setting goals, taking action, collecting feedback, and adjusting strategies with new knowledge—all necessary steps for remaining in tune with market trends and identifying gaps within your organizational structure. The outcome is increased marketing and sales capability that leads to selling more, faster.

Spelled out, FUSE stands for a continuous cycle of Focus, Unite, Sell, and Expand. As Figure 1.1 below illustrates, each iteration increases maturity and customer acquisition. These satisfied customers drive further growth, and the cycle continues and accelerates.

Figure 1.1
(See page 146)

To begin, focus on a stretch sales goal. Stretch goals are ambitious targets that are intended to push teams to perform at their highest levels. A stretch goal should be challenging but also achievable with focused effort and resources. It is used to drive innovation, increase productivity, and promote a culture of continuous improvement. Effective stretch goals have two components: an aggressive sales target and a "make healthcare better" target. Once you have established a stretch goal, your organization's leaders and employees then Unite around that goal and create a GTM plan to achieve it (the action plan). You then Sell, continually improving the offering by collecting customer feedback and iterating each component of the GTM plan. Lastly, Expand involves incorporating that feedback, adjusting your business to achieve better results, and scaling as much as possible by using the replicable processes you've created. The fastest-growing companies update their FUSE GTM plans every 6–12 months.

The output of the FUSE process looks different for every company. This process is not a cookie-cutter formula for success; organizations will differ in their ability to change, the challenges they face, and the expertise they have available. However, for FUSE to be effective in all cases, senior leadership must keep an open mind, commit to active engagement with customers and employees, and listen throughout the entire process. Utilizing the FUSE approach to create a strong GTM plan requires honesty, transparency, and trust for the people within your organization. As you delve deeper into the different aspects of FUSE, begin evaluating your company's true strengths and gaps, and embrace the highly versatile mindset needed to sell more, faster.

THE FUSE GTM PLAN

The key to the "F" in FUSE, Focus, lies in the aggressive goal you establish from the beginning; this goal is critical to aligning your company around a shared vision and measuring your success as you grow. If your GTM assessment reveals where your company currently stands, then your stretch goal reveals how your company wishes to proceed.

It's rare to find companies that have a true vision in mind. Most companies tend to establish short-term goals, such as generating more revenue or reducing costs. The best stretch goals, however, are more ambitious, aspirational, and most importantly, achievable. Think big, but remain realistic. Make the goal as far-reaching as possible while maintaining practicality. Raising annual revenue from $10 million to $50 million over three to five years is a good example. This sales goal is accompanied by a "make healthcare better" goal, such as removing $100 million in cost or eliminating 10,000 medical errors. This is critical so that you are aiming for a higher purpose than just making more money. Don't get me wrong—profit is critical. But you need balance. The goal may seem tough to accomplish, but it's possible with an organized action plan, which will be broken down into steps for your team to execute.

Once a company lands on a suitable stretch goal, we then consider what prohibits the company from reaching it by performing a maturity gap analysis. You compare your company's GTM capabilities to the healthcare technology, software, and service industry's most rapidly growing organizations. From there, determine which areas are adequately developed and which areas need improvement.

The GTM components act as key considerations when identifying a company's strengths, weaknesses, opportunities, and threats (SWOTs) and composing a plan for achieving rapid growth.

The FUSE GTM Maturity Components (Sample Evaluation Criteria)

Value Proposition

- Is your value proposition optimized to clearly answer the Three Whys?
- Can everyone within the company articulate a consistent value proposition?

Offering

- How well do your offerings drive your value proposition?
- Is the product or service being delivered in a way that produces consistent results?

Marketing

- Does your branding and marketing strategy include the ideal customer profile, buying personas, key messages, market segmentation, promotion, pricing, and competitive positioning?
- Have you successfully created a hero's journey for the customer?

Sales

- Has your sales culture been adopted in the company culture as a whole?

- Are you selling with clients rather than to them?
- Do you have a well-defined sales process everyone in the company follows?
- Have you established a revenue machine with specific metrics and targets for analyzing sales performance?
- Are you continuously monitoring your revenue machine and viewing the data from a curious perspective rather than a blaming perspective?

Delivery

- Are you delivering what you promised during the sales process?
- Have you been successful in consistently creating customer evangelists?
- Do you have a replicable methodology?

Enablement Technology

- Do you employ the appropriate sales and marketing technology necessary for automation?
- Have you optimized the technology you currently use, ensuring you're leveraging the potential benefits available to you?
- Are you leveraging analytics to generate insights for marketing and sales performance improvement?

Assess the company's maturity in each of these areas, and develop an effective GTM plan by identifying gaps and the key decisions needed to close them. Each component is graded on a scale, starting with Emerging, then progressing to Basic, Advanced, and Leading. The closer you are to Leading, the closer you are to leading your market.

Emerging, Basic, Advanced, and Leading: The Maturity Levels Explained

Emerging: If an area is Emerging, process standardization does not yet exist, meaning each individual within the company works from their own methodology. Written content and process guidelines have not been created or distributed to employees. The company is obviously doing something to run the business, but the practices are not codified or documented since it's still learning as it progresses. An example of an Emerging marketing component would be if a company has yet to employ a specific marketing team, so its leadership creates a bare-bones website and sends a few sales emails. In this scenario, the company's marketing aspect would function due to individual, independent work, not due to cohesive, systematized practices performed by a group of trained employees.

Basic: The Basic label applies when some thought has gone into developing the component, yet the component is neither well-researched nor refined. At this point, the company has begun putting methods in place, writing operations down, and working on creating a replicable methodology. In other words, a Basic ranking means the component reaches minimum requirements. Most early-stage companies fall somewhere between Basic and Emerging unless they have spent extensive time and effort working to excel. For example, a sales process component is considered Basic if the company's sales team only occasionally collaborates to share best practices, occasionally accesses its Customer Relationship Management (CRM) software, and sells according to personal preferences rather than company-wide, standardized systems.

Advanced: Advanced areas present almost no issues in day-to-day operations. The component is well-documented, efficiently functions, and is understood by all individuals—it hits on almost all cylinders. We rarely see companies with fewer than $50 million in revenue possess more than one Advanced component. Our work generally includes evolving an Emerging or Basic area into an Advanced one, which then aspires to grow into a Leading component over time. Imagine that a company wins a deal and receives positive reviews for its streamlined execution; as a result, its delivery component could be labeled Advanced. With some room for improvement, the company could perhaps implement land and expand training for its employees or better define its customer onboarding process, but for the most part, its delivery component is effectively curated.

Leading: Finally, the Leading designation is reserved for companies that serve as true market leaders. These companies pave the way for others in their industries, and a Leading component is virtually optimized to near perfection. For the companies SalesSparx works with, attaining a Leading component is more of an aspirational, rather than a realistic, goal—at least in the first few years. Take a moment to evaluate Epic Healthcare's value proposition of "one patient, one medical record." In the 1990s, this approach was new and aspirational. Now, "one patient, one record" is an industry-leading value proposition.

EXECUTE YOUR GTM PLAN

Using the GTM plan you created, your organization must then Unite around the actions necessary to achieve the established stretch goal. Unite activities differ from company to company; after all, companies have distinct gaps to fill and goals to reach. No matter the company, every individual within the business should understand each key objective and how their contributions directly impact goal attainment. Every hand on deck should feel a sense of ownership over their responsibilities, which will give them the dedication and concentration they need to drive their individual tasks forward.

SELL, TEST, LEARN, AND ADAPT

Through the execution of the GTM plan, your team transforms their actions into new sales. Alignment, meaning the Unite aspect of FUSE, acts as an essential predecessor to Sell. Sales is a team sport—every function in the company should synchronize with driving customer value and executing internal operations. At this point, all individuals within the organization should be able to follow a shared vision sales process confidently and frequently. The organization should also have sales enablement materials available for staff training initiatives. Finally, account managers should leverage a thorough understanding of their clients' needs and strive to build successful, long-term relationships with customers.

To support the sales activities, SalesSparx's Shared Vision Selling (SVS) process positions buyer and seller collaboration as key inputs to solution and sales model development. SVS, further documented in Chapter Five, establishes behaviors and actions the sales team needs to be successful, thus incorporating the sales culture into the overall company culture. Emphasizing ideation and iterations at every step of the sales cycle, SVS enables companies to sell *with* clients rather than *to* them.

SELL MORE, FASTER

The final aspect of FUSE, Expand, involves sustaining sales success into your company's future. The goal here is to maintain the replicable best practices across the organization, even after the leadership begins to work *on* the business instead of *in* the business. Your process should remain iterative, relevant, and fresh. Clear decision making should become second nature as your company fosters a culture that prioritizes teamwork and customer relationships and leverages sales technology to streamline workflows. Keep your goals top of mind and drive big. Remember, complacency is never an option.

Figure 1.2 illustrates the initial GTM maturity of a typical SalesSparx client. In this example, the delivery, value proposition, and offering GTM components are at or around the basic level, which is the minimum level needed to scale sales rapidly. However, the company's marketing, sales, and enablement technology components have lagged behind and are impeding growth. In other words, the sales are difficult to generate but, once closed, provide great value to the customer. With the less mature components identified, SalesSparx utilizes FUSE iteration to bring them to higher levels of maturity.

Figure 1.2

(See page 147)

As you cycle through each FUSE GTM iteration, your company will be better equipped to achieve market leadership. Typical FUSE outcomes include:

- increasing sales by 20–100 percent in 4–12 months;
- creating a replicable process for the introduction of future offerings;
- improving long-term sales performance;

- strengthening team skills, knowledge, and expertise; and
- maintaining sustainable competitive advantage.

FUSE: An Overview

Focus

- Establish your goals for the future, ensuring they are ambitious yet achievable.
- Perform a maturity gap analysis to identify the SWOTs associated with the GTM components.
- Develop a GTM plan to close the gaps, optimize sales/revenue production, and support rapid 50-100 percent sales growth year over year.

Unite

- Assign accountability for the actions of each team member.
- Ensure every team member feels a sense of ownership over their tasks; everyone should feel prepared to hit the established sales and revenue targets.

Sell

- Execute the planned actions to meet company goals.
- Employ SalesSparx's Shared Vision Selling (SVS) methodology to emphasize ideation and iteration at every stage of the sales cycle and achieve a shared vision.

Expand

- Scale as much as is feasible and sustainable.
- Maintain the replicable process you've created, and sustain the company culture's focus on growth.
- Update your stretch goals and repeat FUSE GTM planning every 6–12 months.

SALESSPARX FUSE CASE STUDY: THE HEALTHCARE IT STAFFING COMPANY

One of the most influential companies that informed SalesSparx's FUSE approach was an industry-leading healthcare IT professional services company that I worked for. The company's initial focus was to hire skilled hospital staff members and place them in other health systems to provide their specialized services. A private equity firm had purchased controlling interest in the company and identified an opportunity for generating a 25–50 percent increase in valuation: the company had to diversify its offerings and enter management consulting. As the company had no management consulting division to speak of, they brought me aboard to enact a strategy and build a team.

Though this project occurred years before the SalesSparx team finalized FUSE, I recognize in retrospect how FUSE served as the main proponent in unifying the sales culture and propelling it to rapid expansion. My main focus became devising a way to leverage the already successful staffing side of the business to generate leads for the solutions sector. My team members and I had to rally around a very aggressive stretch goal, which consisted of growing from $0 to $60 million over three years while, at the same time, "making healthcare better" (Focus). This goal created a compelling vision and helped motivate our team to define high-value solutions that would drive cost savings and improve revenue in a measurable way (Unite). To do so, my team directly interviewed and gained feedback from staffing employees to craft well-informed solutions for existing clients (Sell). This hands-on approach greatly aided us in selling solutions that would impact the largest health system improvement opportunities, cost savings, revenue generation, and regulatory compliance. The final steps required ensuring the company continued preserving and cultivating the replicable process we had created to score even larger gains in the future (Expand).

Through this initiative, our team proved a company can successfully be both a staffing firm and a management consulting firm. The new management consulting division scaled from $0 to $60 million in three years, and the overall company scaled from $50 million to $250 million. We were then able to sell the company to a Fortune 100 company for the largest valuation for any professional services company in our space at the time. Not only did we reach record growth, but we also ranked number one in KLAS, an annual report that highlights exceptional software and services companies, and were voted the best place to work in our industry segment.

CHAPTER TWO

Value Proposition Maturity

CHAPTER SUMMARY

- A value proposition should answer why a buyer needs to change, why they need to change now, and why your company is the right partner to lead them through that change.
- Underpin your proposals with language that connects with emotion and is backed up by facts.
- Leadership and sales teams should all be trained to articulate the proposed value of their offering and how it will be delivered to customers.

In Simon Sinek's book, *Start with Why*, Sinek establishes one question as the driving force behind all success, influence, and progress: "Why?" According to Sinek, customers do not buy *what* you do; they buy *why* you do it. Your organization, of course, was formed to generate profit; that's a "why." However, the "why" Simon proposes speaks to a larger purpose. Why does your organization exist? Does it contribute to a cause? What does it believe?[2] All of these questions lend themselves to developing a dynamic, influential value proposition—the direct answer to "why" a buyer should change what they are doing right now and partner with your company.

Prospects often approach SalesSparx with one question: "Why your company?" Many business leaders respond to this question with an immediate solution and rehearsed elevator pitch, despite not yet understanding the prospect's problem. Rather than recite SalesSparx's value proposition with no clear idea of the customer's needs, my answer is always the same.

"I can't tell you why we're right for you, but I can tell you why our clients have chosen us," I say. "Until we have some conversations about your specific needs, I don't yet know if our capabilities are a fit." I then ask about the buyer's pain points, explain how SalesSparx has helped clients before, and detail SalesSparx's services and past successes. Only then can I determine if the client will gain the most out of their experience with our company. This builds foundational credibility with the buyer as I show that I am not simply attempting to close the sale; I truly care about their outcomes and want to ensure our services are an optimal fit.

The key to crafting a value proposition, then, relies on positioning your buyers and customers as the centers of their own hero's journeys, a branding and marketing cornerstone that I explore further in Chapter Four. In many cases, SalesSparx finds that companies position themselves as the "hero" on the journey rather than the customer. Their value proposition focuses too much on their own brand and understates how they can serve the customer. The two quotes below demonstrate the difference between the two types of value propositions. Ask yourself which company you would prefer to talk to.

"Look at Me" Value Proposition: "We Are Elite Healthcare Consultants!"

"Trusted Advisor" Value Proposition: "Together, Make Healthcare Better"

In addition to proper communication, many companies also struggle with consistency. Your company's value proposition should reach every corner of your organization. Everyone within the company should synchronize their language around the crafted value proposition to explain the company's services. I've encountered scenarios in which I've asked key leaders for their company's value proposition, only to receive multiple different answers. The most prominent issue boils down to the accessibility of training for all levels of the organization. Company leadership often stores the company's value proposition and branding language in their heads, therefore making them unavailable to new hires, salespeople, or other staff members. As a result, these employees cannot wholly articulate the company's value proposition as it was never fully shared with them.

Addressing these gaps requires reevaluating the overall purpose of a value proposition. A value proposition should be a succinct statement that answers why a buyer needs to change, why they need to change now, and why your company is the right partner to lead them through that change. When a buyer engages with your company or your marketing materials, you—and everyone within your organization—should leverage your value proposition to identify their needs, provide a solution, and portray your bigger purpose.

The most important factors of a value proposition, however, point back to Simon Sinek's key question: "Why?" Expanding on Sinek's thoughts, SalesSparx employs the

Three Whys when devising a powerful value proposition:

Why is change needed?

- This question establishes the buyer's principal issues. Maybe their costs are growing at an unsustainable pace. Maybe their growth and market share are challenged. Whatever the case, this first question emphasizes that the company is suffering from either an opportunity cost or direct cost, which motivates the prospect to consider change.

Why change now?

- This question is just as crucial as the first one as urgency drives decision making. If your value proposition only answers the question "Why change?" but not "Why now?" the prospect may delay taking action to handle other competing priorities first. The "now" aspect then becomes a critical component of closing the deal.

Why your company?

- Notice how this question, which spotlights your company, falls last on the list. Remember, the buyer is the hero, not your company. You can only proceed to the final question after thoroughly addressing the client's objectives first. This part of your value proposition is then your place to explain your solutions, differentiate from your competition, and most importantly, emphasize your company's greater purpose.

The first two Whys correlate with the two halves of a successful value proposition: the qualitative half and the quantitative half. The qualitative aspect involves emotional response (Why change?) while the quantitative half reinforces those feelings with facts (Why change now?). Every value proposition should lead with a "hook" that appeals to the buyer's emotions and then end with an appeal to the buyer's logic. Every sale is based on emotion and backed by fact.

QUALITATIVE VS. QUANTITATIVE: TWO VITAL ASPECTS OF YOUR VALUE PROPOSITION

Think back to your last purchase. What emotion drove you to seal the deal? Did you buy the product or service because it made you feel joy? Did it make you feel relieved of a burden? No matter the product or industry, an emotion accompanies every purchase an individual makes. For example, someone could buy a new pair of sunglasses to feel more confident, or a homeowner could enroll in home insurance due to fear of the unpredictable. Along the same lines, emotions drive companies' purchasing decisions as well.

For the purposes of this book, we will focus on the two most influential emotional factors that drive healthcare B2B buying decisions: fear and ambition. Fear manifests itself in many ways. Maybe a company fears legal or financial consequences for a lack of regulatory compliance, or a business leader could fear falling behind the competition. The fear of missing out (FOMO) acts as a significant motivator as well. Your value proposition could present your services as an opportunity that will lead to considerable dividends, compelling the prospect to consider your offer carefully for fear of overlooking a chance for massive payoffs.

Ambition, on the other hand, is the driver of the saying: "If you're not growing, you're dying." As such, revenue growth is typically a primary goal for most companies, though that's not to say we should correlate ambition with greed. More revenue means more success, which enables the company to reach its greater goal of benefitting its industry or society as a whole. Healthcare companies are especially driven by this altruism and wish to make a positive, lasting difference. A healthcare company may strive to create medical devices that inspire worldwide innovation, but they require more funds for product development. Another company may offer ingenious solutions that increase accessibility to medical care, but they need more revenue for a management consulting division to streamline their processes. Every prospect is fueled by a broader desire. The first half of your value proposition should tap into this desire—or the fear of never realizing it—and strike at the company's ideal vision for the future.

Once you have successfully captured the customer's driving emotion, you can then quantitatively address the customer's needs with statistics, costs, and examples of past accomplishments. The quantifiable aspect of your value proposition ensures your solution holds up under scrutiny, though an eye-popping number can sway emotions as well. For this half of the value proposition, SalesSparx employs a value calculator, a tool that provides measurable data for the benefits of each solution. While a company can use the value calculator to establish an economic value proposition, a prospect can also use it to engage with the company's value in a way not previously possible. Figure 2.1 below shows a sample value calculator that can be tailored for individual solutions. Visit www.salessparx.com for additional examples.

Value Components	Do Nothing	With Solution
Cost/Patient/Year	$1,000	$500
Number of Patients	10,000	10,000
Solution Implementation (Months)	12	6
Total Patient Cost	$10,000,000	$5,000,000
Total Savings	N/A	$5,000,000
Solution Cost	N/A	$1,200,000
Return on Investment		417%

Figure 2.1

(See page 148)

Consider a health system struggling with high physician turnover rates. Due to the COVID-19 pandemic, regulatory changes, and insurance-related documentation requirements, physician burnout is at an all-time high. These physicians, who completed medical school to help people and pursue their passion for healthcare, are being overwhelmed with administrative duties, resulting in a severe decrease in mental energy and morale. According to the Association of American Medical Colleges (AAMC), the United States could see an estimated shortage of between 37,800 and 124,000 physicians by 2034—an alarming problem as a substantial generation of people continues to age.[3] Thus, this hypothetical hospital's problem speaks to both an industry-wide and nationwide audience.

Say an IT solutions company offers a software solution that can reduce physicians' administrative burdens. Rather than approach the hospital with a lengthy presentation about how the solution works, the company's value proposition can instead follow the formula outlined above. The company's salespeople may first appeal to emotion by describing the effects of the physician shortage, answering the question: "Why change?" Then, they may follow with the crafted slogan: "Get home for dinner." The following quantifiable evidence can include physician turnover rates, reduced costs, revenue generation, and productivity statistics, thus answering the question: "Why change now?" Finally, the salespeople could finish by detailing their solutions and answering that key question: "Why your company?"

The solution selling process traditionally involves asking open-ended questions to determine a buyer's most pressing needs—an undoubtedly important sales skill to perfect. However, what if you could not only *ask* what keeps the buyer up at night, but also *tell* them what should? The key to a solid value proposition is articulating pains better than the buyer can themselves. What does the buyer fear? What are the buyer's ambitions? Tell the buyer about potential issues they have never considered before. Show them why these pitfalls will be a detriment to their operations and how your product or service acts as a solution, using quantifiable evidence to support your claims.

By the time you walk into the first meeting, you should have conducted enough company and industry research to present the prospect with an opportunity they've yet to consider. This opportunity serves as your initial value proposition and evolves into your combined value proposition as you work with the buyer to address their needs. By the end of the process, you should have a final value proposition—a concise, qualitative and quantitative promise of value that can be shortened to an elevator pitch, elaborated on in a deck, featured in promotional materials, and communicated across the company. Use the sample criteria below to evaluate the maturity of your value proposition. For additional criteria, go to www.salessparx.com.

GTM Maturity Model Analysis: Value Proposition (Sample)

Use of the Three Whys

- Emerging: The value proposition does not clearly answer the Three Whys.
- Basic: Potential answers to the Three Whys are present but not refined.
- Advanced: The value proposition is crafted to answer the Three Whys.
- Leading: The Three Whys messaging is always utilized in the sales process with training in place to reinforce understanding and applications.

Emotion Backed by Facts

- Emerging: The company's value proposition does not engage emotions and is not quantifiable.
- Basic: The company's value proposition has some elements that are emotional or quantifiable.

- Advanced: The value proposition contains both emotional and economic characteristics that can be spoken to and build credibility.
- Leading: The company has a fully quantifiable value proposition that appeals to buyers' emotions and portrays the value driven by solutions. There are sales enablement tools, such as insight stories and value calculators, that complement the value proposition.

Organization-Wide Adoption

- Emerging: The value proposition can only be articulated by leadership and has not been formally documented.
- Basic: Some documentation of the value proposition has occurred, and salespeople can articulate the basics.
- Advanced: The value proposition is well documented and incorporated into some sales enablement materials. Salespeople are educated on it and can utilize it well in the sales process.
- Leading: Training and enablement are in place to ensure that all salespeople, as well as leadership, can articulate the value proposition.

SALESSPARX FUSE CASE STUDY: HEALTHCARE IT SECURITY COMPANY

Healthcare security companies, by definition, help organizations protect their databases and technical information and comply with healthcare-specific regulatory requirements such as HITRUST and HIPAA. Therefore, these companies' customers fear being hacked or not complying with security regulations, which can lead to huge financial penalties. There are plenty of companies that can safeguard organizations against data breaches or help them with compliance—these abilities alone do not differentiate a security business. When working with an IT security client, SalesSparx looked past these standard capabilities, which were the only traits highlighted in the company's value proposition at the time, and recognized what made the company unique: its speed.

This IT security company assisted many organizations with moving their data to the cloud, allowing for much more technical flexibility and productivity in a shorter timeframe than its competitors. The quantitative aspect of its value proposition revolved around how the cloud and the company's speed could spur innovation, provoking buyers to fear missing out on the highly lucrative, streamlined future of healthcare. This FOMO was catalyzed by the introduction of population health systems that enable patients and their doctors to monitor the patients' health without requiring any hospital visits. For an organization to adopt this new technology, however, it must have cloud capabilities. Since access to this software would facilitate better patient outcomes, decrease doctors' and nurses' workloads, and even better, contribute to the greater purpose of healthcare innovations, buyers had a difficult time rejecting the qualitative reasons for hiring the IT security company.

The IT security company's quantitative data only further strengthened its value proposition. In many cases, due to their lack of experience with the cloud and associated regulatory compliance requirements, healthcare organizations adopting these new population health systems were stalled; overall, the systems took anywhere from 10 to 12 months to implement. The IT security company could complete the same amount of work in half the time, accelerating millions of dollars in cost savings. The company represented these savings in simple, measurable statistics. For example, as illustrated in Figure 2.2 below, say a healthcare organization could annually save $1,000 per patient by implementing a population health system. If the organization has 50,000 patients, then the system can save $50 million in one year.

Now, imagine that this organization could achieve these savings in six months rather than 12, spending $100,000 a month for the security company's services. Over 12 months, this generates $25 million in additional savings for an investment of $1.2 million, or around a 2,000+ percent ROI. Even if the organization achieves 25 percent of the projected savings, the ROI is still remarkable.

Value Components	Do Nothing	With Solution
Cost/Patient/Year	$12,000	$11,500
Number of Patients	50,000	50,000
Solution Implementation (Months)	12	6
Total Patient Cost	$600,000,000	$575,000,000
Total Savings	N/A	$25,000,000
Solution Cost	N/A	$1,200,000
Return on Investment		2083%

Figure 2.2

(See page 149)

This is how the IT security company formulated a truly effective economic value proposition. It appealed to fears of noncompliance and FOMO, and it intrigued buyers with ambitions of leading healthcare innovation. Finally, it provided data to support its capabilities and prove how its services could save clients millions of dollars on a quick timeline. After optimizing the value proposition, buyers better resonated with the IT security company's brand, purpose, and services, considerably improving the company's overall close rates and deal size.

CHAPTER THREE

Offering Maturity

CHAPTER SUMMARY

- The real solution to addressing the buyer's pain points is the company's offerings. The offerings should deliver fully on the promises made in the value proposition.
- The solution lifecycle organizes the offerings and services a company provides, and it trains the sales team to speak from a single graphic. A complete offering should have touchpoints in planning, building, implementing change, and optimization.
- An offering must include different levels of service to cater to the diverse needs of buyers. Depending on their needs and capabilities, you can "teach them," "do it with them," or "do it for them."

By starting to answer the buyer's Three Whys, you can build a value proposition that addresses their most significant pain points. The concept of a value proposition is merely a hypothesis, though. While you are able to identify where your "patient" is hurting, an identified value hypothesis doesn't actionably solve any of their problems. Your company's offerings, or the components that drive the value proposition, are the real prescription to address your buyer's pain.

No matter your value proposition, your offerings should align with the promises you make to your buyers. Some software companies' value propositions greatly depend on the customer's ability to act on the insight the solution provides. To deliver the value that they advertise in their value proposition, they must develop training programs to educate end users on how to operate the technology. This is where their offerings (the technology) meet their value proposition (the promise to provide an accessible software solution).

Solutions help buyers overcome a pain point by altering a component of their business. The process of reaching an improved future state via this necessary change typically follows a lifecycle that begins with planning, flows into implementation, and then progresses into continuous improvement. Depending on the type of solution, this lifecycle will contain a range of overall process steps, including training, design, software build/configuration, etc. It is important for a company to understand this entire lifecycle specific to its own offerings.

THE SOLUTION LIFECYCLE

The solution lifecycle graphic in Figure 3.1 represents an example of a full view of the offerings and services that one of our clients provides from strategy to optimization, exemplifying how each one is a single step towards unlocking the full value that the company proposes in its value proposition. This unified view allows a company to introduce new offerings in a way that is informative rather than "salesy," so when the engagement ends, both the buyer and seller know what the next step should be.

Once the seller can address why the buyer wants to change and why now, they can reassure the buyer that they have key qualities to help them along their own hero's journey. The inner four quadrants—practical insight, experienced professionals, strong core values, and a flexible approach—are the pillars of the offering, but they are not the offering itself. The arrow surrounding the graphic shows the actual solutions: what they will do to bring that proposed value to the buyer. This means the company can help clients with strategic planning, developing a roadmap for growth objectives, building systems, and more, all the way to optimization.

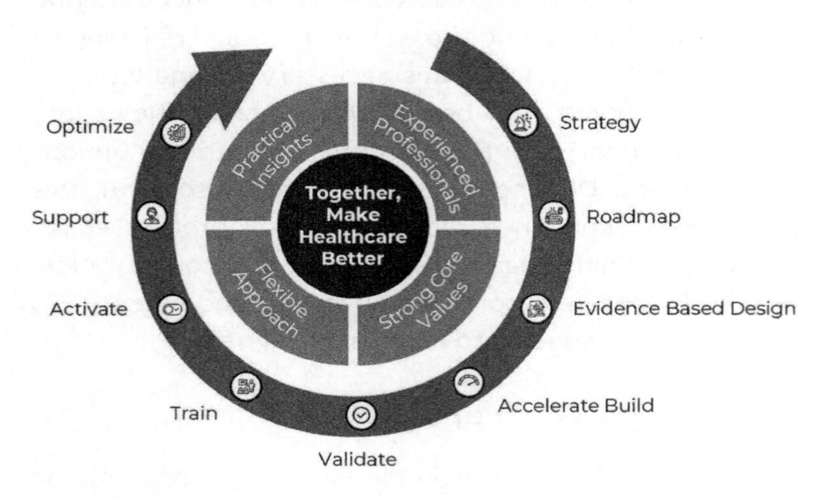

Figure 3.1
(See page 150)

If you can organize your solutions into a solution lifecycle, you can train your sales team to speak from this one graphic. This tool allows SalesSparx to identify if clients' offerings are comprehensive enough for the value they've proposed to their buyers and ask the key question: does their offering run the length of the entire lifecycle? This means the offering must have touchstones of planning, building, implementing the change, and then optimizing it. With an incomplete offering, you aren't addressing all the pieces to generate the promised outcome. A software company, for example, may offer help from planning through training, implementation, and optimization. By touching on all levels of the lifecycle, a complete offering presents itself. Not all of your buyers will need every step of the solution you offer. You can also offer aspects of your solution using partners instead of trying to do it all yourself.

The key to calibrating the lifecycle to a diverse group of buyers is to offer multiple levels of service. Sometimes, a buyer's internal organization is better equipped to handle specific steps within the solution lifecycle. To account for the necessary flexibility in solution delivery, three models, as illustrated by the graphic below, can be used to ensure the most efficient level of value for a buyer's needs.

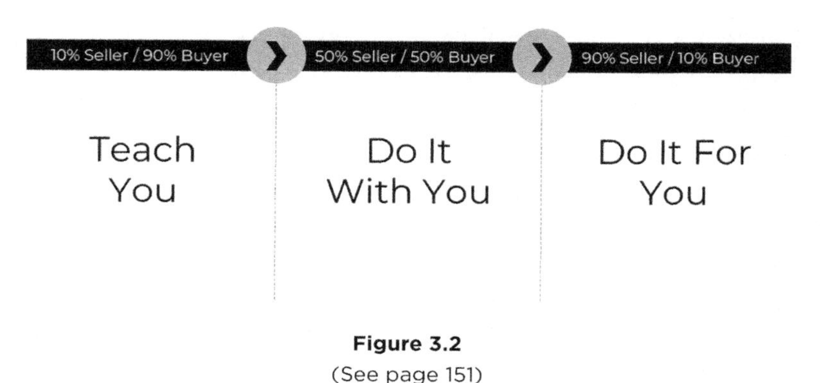

Figure 3.2
(See page 151)

"We'll teach you how to do it."

This model involves the most engagement from the buyer, requiring you to complete 10 percent of the work while they complete 90 percent. This level of consultation provides a solution for your buyer while enabling them to execute the necessary tasks to reach the proposed value you offered them. This offering makes the most sense if the buyer has all of the necessary people and tools to handle implementation, training, and optimization independently.

"We'll do it together."

Collaboration is the key to this model where the work is evenly shared between you and the buyer. A level of teaching must still take place, but your company will be handling a larger part of the solution lifecycle. By working together, the value proposition is realized while the buyer still has some hands-on experience during the solution's integration.

"We'll do it all for you."

In this model, you will perform 90 percent of the work while your buyer performs 10 percent. Here, the buyer needs the solution and all the tools you offer for there to be a successful implementation. For this to benefit the buyer, your lifecycle must be offered in a complete package that covers every step of the solution. In some cases, they may even fully outsource a portion of their business (e.g. revenue cycle or patient enrollment) for a period of time to your company.

Even when the offering is a perfect fit for a buyer, a repeatable methodology must be in place to ensure that the delivered product or service produces consistent results. Say you've developed an analytics software solution that will aggregate clinical and supply chain data, thereby giving the customer insight into their clinical costs and finding opportunities for improvement. If you supply a buyer with the software and then wonder why the buyer doesn't gain any value from it, it's most likely because a specialist needs to teach them how to interpret the new data they received, analyze their operations, and create an action plan for change. This may be out of your company's comfort zone as an analytic software developer, but you either need to teach the buyer how to use it or bring in a partner to walk them through the process (i.e., a consulting or services firm). If there aren't options within your packaged solution, your buyers will never attain their desired results, and your company will not reach its objectives either.

My friend and mentor, Frank Robinson, who coined the term "minimum viable product," addresses this issue of market validation with the phrase: "Nail it, then scale it."[4] You must nail your business model before you can develop criteria for scaling. Those replicable methodologies that allow your customers to have consistent results make up the "nailing" process. There's a difference between nailing a business that meets basic requirements and nailing a business that is ready to scale. An accessible support structure around the core product must be in place that leverages those three value models: we'll coach you, we'll do it together, and we'll do it for you. Companies that offer all three grow the fastest. Once you train everyone in your company on how to talk about the solution lifecycle graphic, then everyone can adopt a unified script for meeting customer needs, though communication training is also essential to ensuring departments remain collaborative.

THE VALUE OF UNIFIED COMMUNICATION

Consistent communication and messaging are necessary across all departments. A major problem companies encounter is when their marketing and sales teams are disunified and not understanding the voice of the customer, or VoC. Everyone should recognize what the offering entails and be able to communicate this with consistent language. All individuals within the company should have the same response to the question: "What is it that you sell?" The key to creating this consistency lies in understanding what the salespeople on the frontlines are experiencing and driving that back into how your offering evolves.

Sales teams often have rich, meaningful conversations with buyers, but unfortunately, the critical information seldom makes it back to management, the marketing department, or the engineers. If you can capture the buyer's voice, no matter what department you are in, the offering will benefit. Include team members outside of sales in these conversations with buyers, or find a way to share these conversations with them so they can have a first-hand account of customer feedback as the customers interact with your product. This is a key reason why fast-growing companies run into more issues than when they were smaller—it is much easier and more likely that frontline information makes its way up the chain with fewer people involved.

More communication makes the voice of the customer more accurate. People on the ground or in other departments often have access to information that salespeople rarely see. That information can be used to adapt the points of emphasis that sales or marketing uses as well as to change the offering to better align with feedback. Figure 3.3 below illustrates the types of information that should be captured in your VoC database.

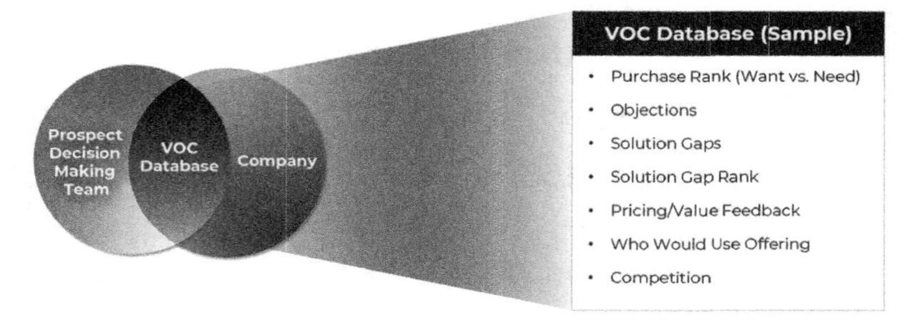

Figure 3.3
(See page 152)

Once communication is unified and the language behind the offering is universal, departments can learn how the services they provide contribute to the whole company. It is not necessary for every person to be an expert in every part of the business; rather, they only need to know the benefits of each additional service beyond their own. Employees are incentivized to learn this due to the potential for cross-selling. For example, if you are placed as staff in an organization and see issues that the solutions department could solve, that information could help your solutions division win a deal. In this case, the staff member simply needed to know the basics of another department's services to create more value for it. If the same understanding is extended on an organization-wide scale, the company has the potential to generate more sales, especially in upselling scenarios. Keep in mind, though: change like this is only possible with an open mind and an affinity for continuous improvement. Use the sample criteria below to evaluate the maturity of your offering. For additional criteria, go to www.salessparx.com.

GTM Maturity Model Analysis: Offering (Sample)

Market Validated

- Emerging: The offering is new and has little to no proven results.
- Basic: The offering has some proven results with some documentation of success.
- Advanced: The offering is proven with multiple strong customer success stories and case studies.
- Leading: The offering has many well-documented success stories and is at the top of its class in terms of results and customer satisfaction.

Solution Lifecycle

- Emerging: There is no defined solution lifecycle; the offering is its own individual entity.
- Basic: Links between the offering and others are informally explained with a suggestion of greater benefits.
- Advanced: The solution lifecycle has touchstones of planning, building, implementing the change, and then optimizing.
- Leading: The seller can clearly explain how all offerings interconnect to bring greater value to the buyer. Solution lifecycle touchstones are integrated into every sale.

Service Level Definitions

- Emerging: The service levels are not clearly defined.

- Basic: The offering has informal service level definitions.
- Advanced: There are defined service levels for each offering (e.g. teach you, do it with you, do it for you).
- Leading: The offering service levels are defined to the buyer, and help is provided to analyze the best choice for their situation.

SALESSPARX FUSE CASE STUDY: HEALTHCARE DATA ANALYTICS COMPANY

One of SalesSparx's clients developed a pioneering analytics tool to help health systems better manage their expensive clinical assets. The tool could be implemented in three to four months and could uncover millions of dollars in cost-saving opportunities. The challenge was that the software by itself could only identify opportunities, not execute on them. There needed to be a focused effort around changing the operations and implementing the recommendations to capture the necessary value.

To address this gap, the company developed a flexible service with the three options: teach it, do it with you, or do it for you. However, our client wanted to remain a software company instead of building a large services organization. They didn't want to evolve their company to provide consulting services. SalesSparx acknowledged their needs and suggested introducing consulting companies to sell and execute these service projects and, in turn, drive substantial cost savings for the health systems. By having the consulting firms approach target buyers, they could pitch a combination of their own services in addition to the data analytics company's software.

In the end, a mutually beneficial relationship formed. The customers reaped the benefits of the software, improving their profitability by millions of dollars. The consulting firm sold highly profitable service projects. And the software company increased sales of their software, creating a win-win-win scenario.

CHAPTER FOUR

Marketing Maturity

CHAPTER SUMMARY

- Marketing is focused on creating demand and the conditions for a sale to scale, whereas sales is focused on closing deals. Marketing and sales must work in lockstep to drive sales, revenue, and growth.
- The buyer's journey is the process a buyer goes through when deciding to change and make a purchase. Understanding the mindset of the typical buyer is key to aligning with them and maintaining their engagement throughout the selling process.
- The seller's job is to act as a guide or advisor to the buyer, providing credible, informative insights that will help the buyer develop trust and confidence in their decision. The seller's unique point of view is a mechanism for differentiation and competitive advantage within their market.
- Thought leadership is critical to this narrative, and brands that prove their value through speaking engagements, content, and optimized marketing materials are more successful than those that simply tell their target audience about their expertise.
- Metrics are important in measuring the effectiveness of the marketing strategy, and the goal is to increase brand recognition within the target market until every targeted buyer can distinguish the brand.

When meeting someone for the first time, the social norm is to introduce yourself, then pivot the conversation to learn more about the other person. For example, say you walked up to a new acquaintance and told them your name. You might ask for their name in return and inquire about them rather than immediately launch into a lengthy explanation of your own interests and personal life. The same principle applies to branding and marketing. As we briefly reviewed in Chapter Two, buyers are not interested in learning about your company objectives and mission unless you position them as the "hero" within their own hero's journey.

The original hero's journey framework was coined and popularized by Joseph Campbell in the 1940s. His famous text, *The Hero with a Thousand Faces*, outlines the template that many narratives follow: a hero, the protagonist of the story, embarks on a quest; overcomes a conflict with the help of a wise, trusted advisor; and returns home permanently transformed.[5] This journey is depicted in Figure 4.1 below.

The Hero's Journey

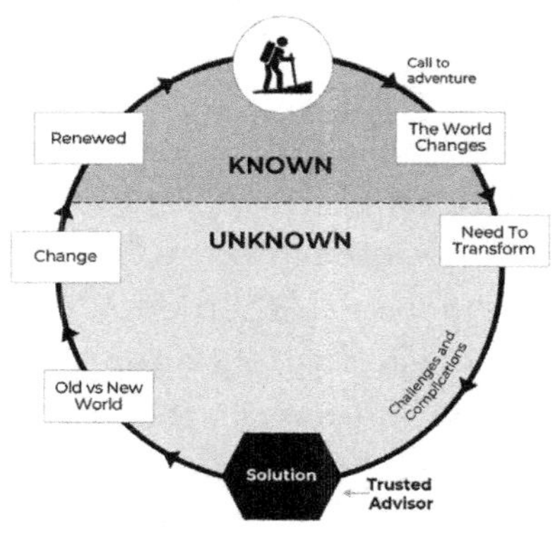

Figure 4.1
(See page 153)

This formula applies to many examples from popular culture—Luke Skywalker, Harry Potter, and Frodo Baggins, to name a few. If your buyer is Luke Skywalker, then your company adopts the role of Master Yoda, acting as a valuable guide and resource for enabling the hero to overcome the obstacles they face.

Thought leadership, then, becomes critical to the hero's journey narrative. As the advisor, you are expected to contribute credible, informative insights that will aid the "hero" in progressing past their conflict. Your company's unique point of view, as a result, becomes a mechanism for differentiation and competitive advantage within your market. Your brand is your company's story, and as with any story, the key is to show *and* tell. Brands that only tell their target audience about their exclusive industry expertise don't succeed as much as brands that prove their value via speaking engagements, thoughtful content (magazine articles, whitepapers, newsletters, etc.), and optimized marketing materials. By contributing to conversations permeating your industry, you build credibility without putting the spotlight on yourself, instead focusing the narrative on your buyers.

THE BUYER'S JOURNEY

In branding and marketing, Campbell's idea of the "hero's journey" directly translates into the "buyer's journey," the process a buyer undergoes when deciding on a purchase and making the decision to change. Understanding the mindset of your typical buyer is the key to aligning with them and maintaining their engagement throughout the selling process. The buyer's journey graphic (featured in Figure 4.2) details the prospect's thought process over time and then matches their questions and needs with appropriate actions for the seller to facilitate the sale.

Figure 4.2

(See page 154)

Buyers follow four pivotal steps along their journey: awareness, consideration, decision, and advocacy. The buying process begins with awareness of your brand, examining if your target audience knows your offering exists and what they already understand about your company. After the awareness stage, buyers then move to the consideration stage where they begin exploring their solution options and conducting research to find the best fit for their needs. A large part of the consideration stage does not only involve finding a solution, but also requires determining if a solution is necessary at all. Progressing to the decision stage means the buyer has determined that their problem is significant enough to undergo the decision-making process and choose the most suitable solution. Finally, the advocacy step occurs when the buyer becomes a brand advocate, openly discussing the success they experienced with your solution with other potential buyers. The advocacy portion of the buyer's journey then leads to other opportunities, which fuels your salespeople to follow the buyer's journey again for the next prospect.

Awareness: Driving Brand Recognition

From a seller's perspective, the awareness stage involves defining your ideal customer profile and then generating leads around your target audience. This involves two types of marketing initiatives: outbound and inbound marketing. Outbound marketing involves heavy advertising, such as commercials, cold calls, marketing emails, etc. In contrast, inbound marketing, or effective thought leadership tactics, acts as a magnet with clients requesting more information about your offerings on their own. Examples include newsletter sign-ups, social media content, and search engine optimization. Though both outbound and inbound marketing materials are essential to your overall strategy, a strong inbound marketing approach not only saves your salespeople time and effort by drawing buyers to you, but it also increases buyer engagement, allowing prospects to interact with your brand and ask questions without feeling pressured or "sold to." There is a lot of discussion that companies can succeed with inbound marketing only, but with complex offerings, this is unlikely to be true. A company needs both inbound and outbound marketing to be successful.

Metrics become increasingly important in this beginning step. Say you know 5,000 organizations exist within your target market, but only 100 of these companies recognize your brand. Month after month, more organizations should gain awareness of who you are and what you do until every group within your market can distinguish your brand. Determining the effectiveness of your marketing strategy depends on first establishing metrics around buyer awareness, identifying how much of this awareness is converting into action, and then optimizing your overall process and messaging to increase engagement continuously.

Consideration: Qualification Criteria for the Ideal Customer Profile

Qualification acts as one of the most important aspects of the buyer's journey. In this stage, sellers use the Four Rights, developed by our partners Mark Rangell and Pete Desjardins at Execullence (www.execullence.com), to determine which target market segments, decision-makers, business problems, and triggering events can best accelerate profitable revenue growth.

The Four Rights

1. **Right Organization:** What industry segment or type of company are you targeting? How large is this company, how many employees do they have, and how much revenue do they generate?
2. **Right Persona:** Who are the major decision makers within the organization? What is the optimal strategy for connecting with them and building a relationship? Do they have the authority to make a decision?
3. **Right Timing/Triggers:** What external factors could influence the target organization to consider your offerings? Is the company facing regulatory changes, hiring new leadership, or

expanding into new markets? Do they have the necessary budget?

4. **Right Pain Points:** What pain points are the organization seeking help with, and what new pain points can you help them recognize? Though many pain points will be identified through conversations with the client, you can diagnose more from available databases to see if they are having quality, cost, market share, regulatory, or other challenges.

After developing each qualification criteria, you can then reexamine past deals you have closed to find the target audience that best correlates with your offerings. What organizations are an okay fit, and which were the best fit? Who were the best people to contact and build relationships with? What triggers allowed you to gain more traction than you would have otherwise and answered the question: "Why now?" Did your offering create measurable value?

Adjusting your target buyer based on these questions greatly reduces the amount of time you spend on prospects who are not a fit. Remember, qualification does not end once you decide on an ideal customer profile; you must continually ask these questions as your company scales, strengthening each area and revisiting each criterion as you learn more and the market evolves. Figure 4.3 below is an example of a Four Rights scorecard, developed for a healthcare IT consulting firm's EHR Help Desk offering. The scoring of each area may be weighted differently for each offering and typically totals 100. The scoring is as much art as it is science—do not feel concerned if one prospect is an 85, and another is an 80 or even 75. Though, do look for major gaps like a 90 versus a 60. This tool allows you to determine which prospects to focus on, based on whether they are not a fit, a workable fit, or a complete fit.

Category	No Fit	Workable Fit	Complete Fit	Score
Right Customer	• Full outsourced effective Help Desk solution • Full EHR staff with free time - able to resolve all issues in a timely manner	• Small groups (20-50) with low Help Desk staff • Limited after-hours su pport	• Large independent groups (50-250+) with no staff time • Epic/Allscripts/Cerner • Excessive ticket/call volume	0-15
Right Persona	• Non-Management • Analyst	• VP • Director • Physician	• Application VP • CIO • CIMO • CFO	0-30
Right Pain Points	N/A	• Low staff retention • Future projects gaps • Not enough staff to adequately support providers	• Not meeting current SLAs • High operational cost • No proactive/trending issues analytics • High end user dissatisfaction rates	0-25
Right Triggers	N/A	• Patient/physician satisfaction initiative • Quality of care grade drop	• Upcoming EHR switch • Help Desk RFP	0-30

Figure 4.3

(See page 155)

Though deal execution obviously leads to revenue generation, the buyer vetting process remains essential to determine if the buyer will gain value from your offerings. Then, once you determine that your solution will appropriately meet their needs, both parties can progress to ideation to discuss how much value you can deliver and how.

Marketing, as with almost all the concepts covered in this book, also revolves around the Three Whys: why change, why now, and why your company? Whether you are optimizing your value proposition, offerings, or another core aspect of your business strategy, the Three Whys serve as fundamental questions to answer for consistent brand messaging and value delivery.

Marketing is no different—if you do not curate a clear message surrounding why your buyer should change their practices or why they should change now, you most likely will not have a fully honed branding and marketing GTM component.

The consideration stage addresses this, answering the buyer's question: is there enough value to justify the effort? Standing out from similar offerings in your market requires defining your specific benefits. The Three Whys provide a streamlined way to present your value while also achieving differentiation from your competition. You may feel compelled to share the outstanding data you have collected and positive feedback from past clients while ideating with potential buyers. However, the consideration stage is for addressing the buyer's needs; you must also present your prospects with novel and engaging ideas that appeal to *their* objectives. The companies that differentiate themselves in this way are the ones who win. Epic, Amgen, and Stryker—each of these companies' leaders paved the way by building their brands around thought leadership and a value-first mindset.

Decision: Developing Well-Researched Proposals and Pricing

Once you have spent an adequate amount of time—that is, enough time to understand the buyer's pain points—you can then present the prospect with a proposal of services. Due to the time you and the buyer spent on ideation, this proposal then transforms the seller's proposal into the buyer's proposal. If the buyer feels significant ownership of the solution by the time they receive the proposal, it will be signed more quickly. Nailing your proposal on the first try in this way can save the deal from months of back and forth with the buyer. You want to make sure that their ideas are reflected in the final document and phrased in a way they best connect with. When properly executed, you should see 50–70 percent or more of your proposals accepted.

Any deal also involves some level of negotiation, whether that is over contract terms and conditions or pricing. Effective negotiation requires establishing value as early as possible. If the buyer recognizes the value of your offerings and understands the ROI they will receive, their chances of prolonging negotiations decrease. The steps of the seller process set you up for portraying this value; however, attaining your desired contractual outcomes markedly depends on assessing your competition and fortifying your pricing model.

Understanding your competition and how you favor in the market enables your company to define its individual qualities and set a profitable, yet justifiable, price. This necessary understanding stems from in-depth market research, utilizing online tools, and even tactics like secret shoppers, if applicable. This research can then be used to develop company battle cards for illustrating competitive differentiators and competitors' key strengths. If you own Coca-Cola, you know for a fact that you will run into Pepsi, so how do you tailor your brand to ensure that soda drinkers know how you differ? Resources like competitive battle cards distinctly outline all of your company's and competitors' qualities to ensure everyone within your company, especially your marketing and sales departments, can articulate these differences using the same language.

This competitive understanding also enables you to set the highest price possible. Many companies establish their pricing around their costs; if they want to make a certain amount of profit, then they will factor in how much it costs to deliver their offering and adjust the price accordingly. Though this method does generate a practical price, it neglects to consider the value your organization creates for the buyer. Your company's value could add on around 10–50 percent more profit if correctly incorporated into your price and justified via sales materials. Say a business's solution costs around $50,000 to deliver. We often see companies designate their price as $100,000. However, this assessment may leave money on the table; in actuality, their offering could be producing a million-dollar benefit for their buyer. Given that this company can explain this value to buyers and validate their reasoning, they could easily evaluate their offering price at $150,000.

Advocacy: The Buyer As a Marketing Champion

As the final stage, advocacy finalizes the overall sale and establishes buyer expectations. Advocacy acts as the next steps phase with buyers, communicating clear success metrics and service process details for when you begin delivering on your promised offerings. During this time, buyers may have questions such as "What should I expect?" and "How will my company communicate with the seller to make decisions?" Before progressing to working with the buyer, a seller should reiterate what success looks like and understand how to best communicate with your company on meeting those success measures.

Establishing brand advocates, past or current customers who spread word of your brand and recommend your services to others, is a critical piece to any marketing model. These advocates advertise your brand and generate new leads in an entirely independent manner. In addition, these individuals may continue this advocacy long after you finalize their project, making them invaluable long-term resources. Your level of service and the quality of project deliverables do factor into your overall success here; however, the secret to gaining brand advocates boils down to relationship building. The professionals and organizations you work with care about efficiency and timely completion, but at the end of the day, buyers wish to cultivate beneficial connections that help them achieve their broader goals of improving society or advancing humanity in some way. With your offerings acting as avenues to reach these goals, your buyer is much more likely to become a brand ambassador, accelerating your marketing efforts to new, industry-defining levels.

Sales and Marketing Collaboration

At SalesSparx, we help our clients see marketing and sales as two sides of the same coin, or in other words, both departments typically report to one leader with sales leaders prioritizing marketing and sales enablement initiatives. However, some companies have sales and marketing as two separate departments that are not fully coordinated and focused on the same outcomes. I am not implying that marketing and sales are the same, but marketing largely exists to drive more sales. Some companies overly focus on exhaustive business planning, market studies, competitive analysis, or other marketing activities, and as a result, they do not sufficiently prioritize areas like thought leadership content, sales enablement, or lead generation to support sales. The key is to keep marketing connected to the buyer. If the marketing function does not consistently interact with the sales function, then marketing, the team responsible for sales enablement and lead generation, becomes disconnected from sales. Ground-level feedback should always inform marketing strategy, just as communication materials should always accurately reflect the sales process. The two processes flourish when they are in lockstep.

When SalesSparx partners with a company experiencing a disconnect between sales and marketing, a significant and unfortunately common issue, we focus efforts around informing staff on a unified marketing/sales process and enabling communication through account and opportunity win plans, which you can find an example of on www.salessparx.com. In addition, we also identify disruptions along the sales pipeline by reviewing the buyer's journey. If most deals abruptly end in the qualification stage, then we can establish a plan for reevaluating the Four Rights and better defining their target buyers.

Similarly, many companies falter in the awareness phase as they do not utilize mechanisms for capturing market feedback, thereby impacting the following steps of the seller process. These organizations fail to ask their audience the right questions or try new strategies for capturing the voice of the customer. SalesSparx often tackles these issues through new technology integration or leveraging unused features of already used software. For example, a standard customer relationship management (CRM) tool can be employed to compile basic information, such as the typical objections clients propose, the way clients react to your value proposition, what additional services clients request, and reasons for deal loss. Capturing this information and then disseminating it at an organization-wide level allows different parts of the company to further understand and participate in the sales process.

Another important concept in the integration of sales and marketing is mapping the buyer's journey to the SalesSparx SVS process described in Chapter 5. Figure 4.4 shows a sample of this mapping.

Buyer Journey To SVS Process Map - Sample

Buyer's Journey	Awareness	Consideration			Decision		Advocacy
Buyer Objectives	• What are others doing? • How do I define the problem? • What are possible solutions?	• What solutions are available? • What is the value of a solution? • What can I learn on my own?	• Is this a "need to have" solution? • What will others on the team think? • What is in this for me?	• Will it work in our organization? • How can I ensure all stakeholders are aligned? • Is there enough value to justify the solution?	• Can I meet with others that have used the solution? • Help me justify the cost relative to the value. • Have we met all of our decision criteria?	• Navigate internal purchasing process. • Have we addressed all regulatory and legal concerns?	• What do I expect? • How will we ensure success? • How will we measure value? • How will we communicate internally and make decisions?
Enablement Materials	• Contact Database(s) • Contact Cadence • Case Studies • Customer Testimonials • Interactive Value Calculator • Explainer Videos • Whitepapers	• Lead Scoring (4 Rights Criteria) • Objections and Objection Handling (by persona) • Initial Business Value Calculator (by solution type) • Competitive Battlecards • Intro Presentations • Buyer Journey maps	• Discovery Checklist • Pain Point to Solution Mapping • Ideation Document Template • Business Value Calculator • Maturity Model • SVS Playbook	• Ideation Document Example(s) • Ideation Workshop Agenda • Solution Pricing Model • Insight Stories	• Proposal Template(s) by Solution Type • Contract Template(s)	• Negotiation Strategies • Final Objections and Objection Handling	• Sample Customer Success Criteria • Sample Quarterly Business Reviews
Seller Objectives	• Determine account target (suspect) list based on Ideal Customer Profile • Generate engagement • Generate Marketing Qualified Leads (MQLs) • Generate Outbound Qualified Leads (OQLs)	• Determine "fit" with Qualification Criteria • Select initial insight stories • Develop initial value proposition • Determine single sales objective (opportunity level)	• Develop the Coach • Identified solution priorities • Select Pursuit Team	• Confirm Why Change, Why Now, Why Us? • Define product fit • Develop Ideation Document	• Jointly developed, differentiated vision and solution • Combine buying emotion with compelling business case • Refine Shared Vision	• Develop negotiation strategy and tactics • Win-win business arrangement • Finalize Shared Vision • Contract signature	• Customer success • Develop delivery plan • Execute Shared Vision • Identify add-on business opportunities / account growth
SVS Process	Awareness	Qualification	Discovery	Ideation	Proposal	Negotiate	Partnership

Figure 4.4

(See page 156)

As you can see, at the intersection of each stage of the sales process and the buyer's journey, key sales enablement tools are created so that the sales team can drive a consistent message and optimize their ability to collaborate with the buyer. Use the sample criteria below to evaluate your marketing maturity. For additional criteria, go to www.salessparx.com.

GTM Maturity Model Analysis: Marketing (Sample)

Ideal Customer Profile

- Emerging: Ideal customer profiles and buying personas are undefined and individual to each salesperson's assumption.
- Basic: Ideal customer profile definitions have been communicated to sales but with small amounts of detail and formal documentation.
- Advanced: The ideal customer profile is formalized and detailed for every offering. It is used as a guide for lead generation by both marketing and sales.
- Leading: The ideal customer profile is formal and detailed and has enablement materials tailored to each profile. There are defined sales actions and strategies that have been proven effective in engaging each profile.

Buyer's Journey

- Emerging: The buyer's journey is not defined or documented.
- Basic: The idea of the buyer's journey is communicated with a rough outline of buyer and seller objectives throughout the sales process.
- Advanced: The buyer's journey is formally defined from awareness to partnership. There are defined objectives and actions for each stage.
- Leading: The buyer's journey is well-defined, communicated, mapped to the sales process, and

codified in CRM. Tracking the stages is easy for leadership, and salespeople have specific, easily accessed guidance for each stage.

Sales Enablement

- Emerging: There are little to no sales enablement tools in place.
- Basic: Some sales enablement tools are available with informal training to help with utilization.
- Advanced: The company has strong sales enablement in place to support each stage of the buyer's journey with formal training to help with utilization.
- Leading: The company has proven sales enablement tools that evolve from the voice of the customer with strong training programs in place.

SALESSPARX FUSE CASE STUDY: ELECTRONIC HEALTH RECORD CONSULTING FIRM

An EHR consulting firm had "look at me" marketing. The company's website exclusively included copy that praised its services and spoke on its history—very little material represented potential buyers or their pains. The salespeople's pitch, a 20-slide presentation, began with six slides detailing their company and contributions before finally addressing the buyer around slide seven. Despite this, the consulting firm continued to interest buyers . . . yet conversations often struggled to progress.

The firm's salespeople began receiving better reactions and more conversions when they realigned their messaging around what was important to their ideal customer profile, as opposed to what was important to the consulting firm. Their website produced more leads, and more buyers moved on to the next step after viewing their introductory presentation. They began documenting and acting on the voice of the customer, asking questions such as, "Which of our offerings most resonate with your pains, and which offerings do not?" Their salespeople evolved from lecturers to advisors in the buyers' eyes. Though the consulting firm continues to strengthen its overall branding and marketing strategy, these simple adjustments produced great initial success. Most importantly, buyers felt motivated to see them as trustworthy, knowledgeable leaders throughout their individual journeys. During our 12-month partnership with the company, their web traffic and pipeline doubled. The improvements in branding and sales process helped them close the two largest deals in company history and added $30 million to their exit to a major private equity firm.

CHAPTER FIVE

Sales Maturity—Culture, Model, and Process

CHAPTER SUMMARY

- The fastest growing companies create a shared vision with the buyer during the sales process. The SalesSparx Shared Vision Sales (SVS) process is structured to scale sales and prevent bottlenecks.
- A progressive sales culture needs to permeate the sales team and the rest of the company to create a consistent approach to closing deals.
- The Three Whys build successful long-term relationships with customers by selling with them, not to them. The SVS sales process facilitates this collaboration, shortens the sales cycle, and improves sales rates.
- Discovering personal buyer's journeys and empathy will build positive relationships to maximize trust and transparency.
- Ideating alongside a buyer and proposing a plan built with their input creates win-win solutions for everyone. When executed correctly, the proposal has become the buyer's proposal as much as the seller's proposal.
- With proper and respectful negotiations, a long-term partnership can form and continue to grow, cultivating repeat business.
- The identification of the right coach to support the sales process in the buyer's organization is the number one predictor of deal success.

The overall arc of SVS builds the confidence of a buyer through the sales process, guiding the buyer to successful change.Sales teams vary in size, even within multimillion-dollar companies. Not every organization develops large-scale sales departments. Sometimes a few members of leadership work 80 hours per week to drive sales by pounding the pavement, hosting meetings, and converting potential buyers into customers. While their initiative can be seen as admirable, it is not scalable whatsoever. Structure needs to be in place to share best practices, prevent bottlenecks, and promote growth. Business leaders who insist on independently conducting sales miss out on key development opportunities. Scaling a business is impossible without a sales team that can close business on its own.

A progressive sales culture must permeate the sales team, as well as the rest of the company, to create a consistent approach to closing deals. This includes how you hire a salesperson for your organization. They need to recognize and understand a buyer's issues while teaching them about your offerings. Every salesperson needs to establish trust, empathize with buyer pain points, and guide them through the buyer's journey; they need to be credible, reliable, and honest.

Establishing that culture requires a unified sales process, though—one that empowers the buyer to take ownership of the final result. The key to building successful long-term relationships with buyers is by selling *with* them, rather than *to* them. SalesSparx's Shared Vision Sales (SVS) process facilitates collaboration with buyers and, in turn, shortens the sales cycle and improves sales rates. By emphasizing ideation and iteration at every step of the sales cycle, a partnership can be achieved before the deal is closed. Once the process is standardized, your business can focus on accelerating growth and improving predictability.

All of this comes together in SVS's four guiding principles:

Sell solutions and value—not a product or service.

- Every customer has their own personal pain point. Understand that pain and collaborate to ease it rather than provide a one-and-done cure-all. Your product is not just another sale to the buyer, but rather a solution to their problems.

Meet buyers where they are to create a roadmap for success.

- The key to understanding buyers' pain is a matter of perspective. What is standing in the way between where they are now and where they want to be? How can you help remove those roadblocks?

Position your company as a thought leader and guide.

- Your offering holds real value with the possibility to make a positive difference. If you believe your product is the best solution to a problem, share that knowledge in a way that enables your buyers and builds trust.

Set proper expectations to create long-term customer evangelists.

- Buyers may come to you with the hopes of a quick fix, but oftentimes, the solution design requires an iterative process. Clearly communicate this with customers. When they do finally obtain the proposed value, they'll be more likely to share word of your company.

These principles were developed with an important mindset: "Every sale is a decision to change." Change in healthcare is especially complex, having to navigate regulations, patient preferences, physician practice differences, and technological changes. Buyers are looking to make continuous improvements in themselves, working towards their own stretch goals. By operating from the four principles and following the SVS architecture, you can guide your buyers to successful change.

SHARED VISION SELLING ARCHITECTURE

The overall architecture of SVS builds the confidence of a buyer through the sales process. They often begin their buyer's journey unaware of the problem they are facing; your marketing may be what makes them aware of your company and their problem. During this time, prospective buyers haven't made up their minds, but they will begin to ask the Three Whys: why change, why now, and why your company? By the time the partnership has been formed and the deal is done, they'll be able to answer the Three Whys and ready to recommend you to other potential buyers, perpetuating the cycle.

The Three Whys are the engine for this cycle, and by moving through the seven stages, you will help your buyer generate better answers to the questions. Be careful not to force answers on them as they must be the ones to come to conclusions on their own. This protects their sense of ownership over the process and the final offering. With a better understanding of why they are changing, why now, and why your company, the buyer and you will be able to communicate around this shared vision. Figure 5.1 describes the SVS process beginning at the top with awareness and progressing to partnership. Once a partnership is established, SVS is used to "land and expand" and support long-term relationships.

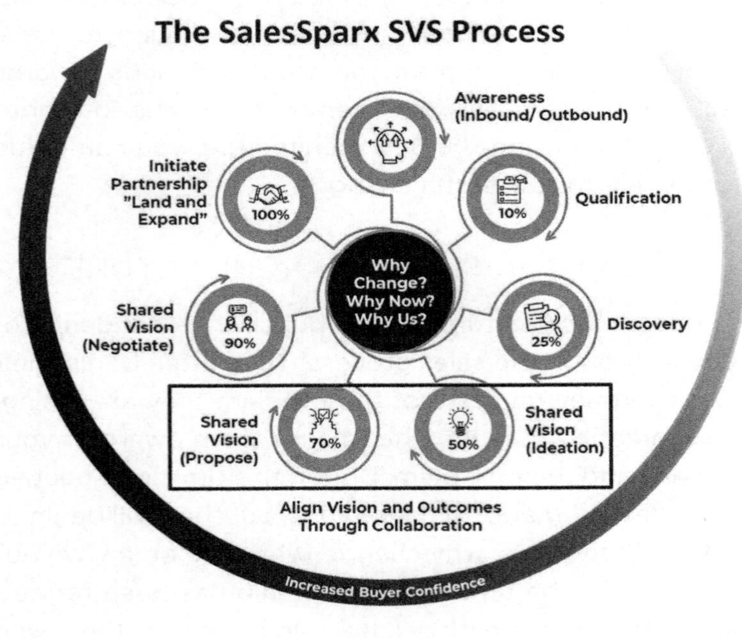

Figure 5.1
(See page 157)

Even though the entire process generates insights and a sense of ownership from the buyer, the most important steps are the third and fourth stages: discovery and ideation. Together, discovery and ideation form the shared vision, giving the buyer confidence in you and your organization. By positioning your company as a source of competitive edge, you become part of the buyer's view of the future, indispensable to their success.

Before moving from one stage to the next, make sure to note your progress. Have you gathered all the information you need to move forward? Is your prospective buyer on the same page as you? Your exit criteria should identify your preparedness to enter the next stage; by slowing down to take stock, you may be saving yourself from losing a deal. You and your prospect should be in sync from when they first become aware of you to signing the contract.

SVS Stage One: Awareness

The awareness stage is focused on targeting healthcare organizations to familiarize them with your company and its offerings. It's key to develop your ideal customer profile so your inbound and outbound activities reach the right prospects. Inbound activities use your website and social media to attract new buyers, prompting them to contact you independently. Outbound marketing uses email and the phone to reach out to target accounts. 100 percent of the people who do *not* know about you are *not* going to buy from you.

Using your ideal customer profile, identifying a manageable target audience of buyers will feed your outbound marketing. Awareness-generating activities turn targeted accounts into marketing qualified leads (MQLs). MQLs meet your ideal customer profile, are engaged with your company, and most importantly, have agreed to meet with the sales team. Once the first meeting has been set, responsibility for the lead transitions from the marketing team to the sales team, and you can begin qualifying them as a buyer. Nailing the awareness stage generates many at-bats for the sales team, directly impacting your company's total sales and revenue performance.

During this earliest stage, communication efforts should be coordinated between marketing and sales. One common language should unify the buyer's journey; between marketing and sales materials, pain points and solutions should be talked about with the same severity to match the proposed value. By monitoring marketing metrics, your teams will be able to determine what language is most efficient in converting prospects into MQLs.

SVS Stage Two: Qualification

The goal of the qualification stage is to determine if you and your prospect are compatible. The best way to measure this process is to make sure you're using the Four Rights: the right organization, the right persona, the right pain points, and the right timing. Unlike the ideal customer profile, which is a set of criteria that can be answered "yes" or "no," the Four Rights often include subjective answers you'll use to determine whether you and the prospect can create a shared vision.

To prepare for this stage, have insight stories about how your company added value for a customer with similar pain points. Also, investigate proprietary databases or public sources to determine what keeps your prospects up at night—or what *should* be keeping them up at night. Doing this homework up front is a foundational step to building credibility and trust, all necessary to form a shared vision of success.

Additional goals to the qualification stage are to both inspire and understand the buyer. Inspiring the customer with your offering gives them the necessary excitement to discuss the potential partnership internally at their company. Understanding allows you to empathize and allocate resources to help the pursuit of the buyer's goals. It also helps you prioritize your time and expertise on the deals with the most business value and the highest opportunity to close.

Confirm the buyer's pain points before moving on to the discovery stage. This will define your single sales objective and qualify the company as a sales lead. Proficient execution of the qualification stage weeds out dead ends that can clog the sales pipeline. This way, sales teams can focus on learning more about the best revenue-generating prospects. With the best prospects identified, look at a potential timeline for their sales process.

SVS Stage Three: Discovery

The discovery stage is where you immerse yourself in the world of your healthcare buyers. Having clarity on their personal wins, key stakeholders, and pain points is critical to a successful discovery stage. Knowing where they are on their change journey enables you to better empathize with their situation—to understand their vision—and move them from where they are to where they want to be. The more you learn about your prospects, the easier it is for the both of you to answer the Three Whys and transition into ideation.

Through this stage, you should also be able to confirm the value that you can bring to them. Depending on the technical aspects of your offering, that unified language between sales enablement and solution architects will ensure that your sales force can generate enough value to wow the prospect. The value you can provide should not be undervalued, though. A major part of discovery is understanding the buyer's steps to buy as well as their *ability* to buy. It is crucial to find the person or people who have the ability to authorize the deal and not waste time if there is no way to allocate budget to your solution.

Your sales team and the prospective buyers will build a relationship over time. Identify the right "coach" within the buying organization who has the potential to turn a tough sell into a near-guaranteed win. Coaches are those who can provide insight into how you can best deliver and present value to those with purchase authority. Opportunities with a distinguished, helpful coach are much more likely to close than those without. They are key allies in being able to nail the shared vision. Generally, we recommend that you do not exit the discovery process without having a coach to help you move the deal forward. Based on an analysis of more than 15,000 SVS sales opportunities, the identification of the right coach in the buyer organization is the number one determinant of deal success.

Data collection should occur throughout SVS, but it is most critical to secure information during the discovery stage. This is the last checkpoint before plunging into the ideation and proposal stages; having as much data about your prospect as possible will help to create a wider, richer shared vision that speaks to their pain points.

SVS Stage Four: Ideation

As you enter the ideation stage together, you and your prospect have progressed toward agreeing on why change is necessary, why change needs to happen now, and why your company is the right partner. Armed with information about the current state, pain points, and desired future state, you and the buyer can leverage the ideation document to discuss how to move them forward. The information you gathered in the discovery stage will make up the initial draft of the ideation document; this document will then be iterated through the ideation stage. By identifying the prospective buyer's pain points and understanding the answers to their Three Whys, you can then help propel them to their ideal future state, even expanding their outlook of the future. Figure 5.2 below is a sample progression we developed for a precision medicine company to show their sales team how information would progress from discussions in the discovery stage through the ideation stage leading to a proposal. Each company will have a different path to follow for their offering and ideally train their sales team on how to facilitate these discussions.

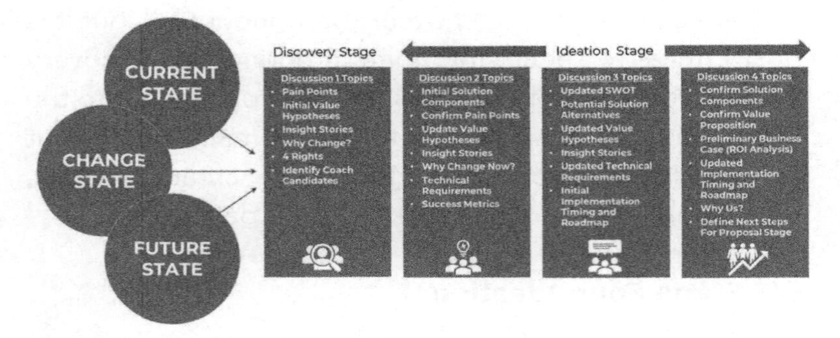

Figure 5.2

(See page 158)

Your job is not to sell them a solution, but to enable their decisions that bring them the most value—again, to sell *with* the buyer, not *to* them. Your company becomes their source of competitive advantage to improve patient care, increase market share, and reduce costs. By bringing new ideas and value, you will build the buyer's trust and confidence in your company as well as their own. This is a heavily buyer-focused time, so there will be plenty of information to capture, guiding the rest of the sales process. After the ideation is complete, you should be able to fully articulate the value of the solution. Ideally, you can quantify improvements in revenue, costs, market share, or speed to market.

This is the most important stage in the sales process for building trust in you and your solution. Through a collaborative process, both you and your prospect will be investing yourselves into how their future will look; every time you meet with the prospect, you'll be updating the ideation document. These notes will begin as rough ideas, but through refinement and continuous improvement, you'll have a complete picture of their path forward. Gain feedback from your coach as they can inform you on what elements of the deal are most vital. Done correctly, the ideation stage leads to closing six to seven out of every 10 proposals, showcasing the power of a shared vision.

To maximize the prospective buyer's ability to picture integrating your offering into their company, your delivery team should align with your sales team during this ideation stage. This means including them during these ideation meetings because they can provide more insight on solutions to the prospect. Delivery teams are aware of all the various scenarios of how your product can be used, and this, in turn, will influence your proposal.

SVS Stage Five: Proposal

The proposal stage is focused on refining the shared vision. The ideation is the foundation of the proposal, and additional details are added to increase alignment. Ensure that the buyer's personal and business wins are addressed while also including a clear economic value proposition. At this point, the buyer should feel more ownership of the solution than your company. You and your prospect have mapped their path to your shared vision, but you must remember they are the hero in this journey. That ideation document will encapsulate the shared vision and naturally become the proposal.

A proposal meeting is designed to review the project scope, approach, major assumptions, work plan, and pricing. All of these need to be aligned within your team before the actual proposal. The presentation should be eye-catching and easy to follow; it should feel familiar to them as it is the shared vision you have been building together. It's a reminder of their potential return on investment from choosing your solution to obtain a competitive edge. Don't forget to check in with your coach and continue to nurture that relationship. Their input will help with your alignment on the final proposal.

Every buying decision is emotional but also backed by data and facts. You appeal to the heart, but you also give the mind something to base its decision on. In the proposal presentation, be sure to reinforce the emotions driving the sale. The two most powerful emotions are fear of loss and hope for gain. With a powerful sense of ownership over the proposal, a prospect should be feeling both: fear of losing out on this opportunity to scale and hope for all the future benefits that come from a successful scale.

While developing pricing, be sure to frame the proposal as an investment in the agreed-upon future, rather than a price. You are providing them with value and potential for their company's future. Generally, 60–70 percent of all your proposals should be accepted. If they are not, then there is likely an issue with your discovery or ideation stages, and the buyer either does not feel ownership or see the full value.

SVS Stage Six: Negotiation

The negotiation stage is key to protecting the value of the solutions and services that your company provides. With SVS, negotiation is usually much easier because of the buyer-seller alignment developed in the ideation and proposal stages. The mark of an optimized negotiation stage is that all parties believe they are receiving excellent value, a true win-win situation.

With SVS, most deals are won or lost in the ideation stage. The negotiation stage is where you make sure everyone can agree to a win-win scenario. Remember what's important to the buyer and what's important for your company; a shared vision ties them together. By prioritizing the overlap in this relationship, it's impossible not to see long-term wins for both organizations.

However, this stage is a matter of ensuring the correct amount of compensation for the value your company provides. Be respectful of proposal feedback and explore accommodations, but don't let the value of your solution be undermined. Your product is the key enabling factor in this shared vision you have both created. If they walk away, they will lose the opportunity to reach their main objectives.

Once the deal is near to close, you want the delivery team to initiate onboarding as soon as possible. This not only helps with fulfillment, but also creates a sense of momentum that pushes the close forward. As soon as the deal closes, the now-customer will have a prompt delivery and proper expectations on timing. If the shared vision process has been executed well, the negotiation stage can be quite rapid as you and the buyer will easily agree on the benefits and proposed value.

SVS Stage Seven: Partnership

In this final stage, you'll have either won the deal—which we hope will happen most of the time—or you'll have closed it as a loss. If the latter is the case, you'll need to document the reason for this loss and apply this data to future sales. If it was a successful sale, though, your next task will be driving long-term customer success. While signed agreements are the *end* of the process for a specific sales opportunity, it is the *beginning* of the relationship in the eyes of the customer. The transition to delivery is completed, and from this point forward, your company's success is determined by how well it executes the expectations articulated during the sales process. The focus is to create customer evangelists!

Once you're in an account, you should be able to continue to add value and accomplish what we call "land and expand." That strong relationship forged in the sales process should extend well into the future, growing along the way. All previously set expectations should be seen as temporary; the objective at this stage is to now exceed them. With every new customer, it is key to continually update the success measures of the partnership and report back on progress.

Partnership is the ultimate goal of the SVS process. By setting the correct expectations prior to the close, the buyer will be delighted by the delivery of your solution and seek to engage you again in the future. In subsequent sales opportunities, you will be able to leverage all the information you have gathered to expand the account far into the future. If you are able to continue to provide them adoptable solutions, you are creating value for them. That value should be reflected accordingly in both of your business plans.

After a smooth sales process, buyers should see you as a trusted advisor and a source of their competitive edge. As a converted customer evangelist, they will hopefully give you quotes and stories to incorporate into your marketing to help with future buyers. Positive word of mouth cannot be underestimated as they may speak highly of you to their peers.

SALES CULTURE AND HIRING

Sales culture and hiring go hand in hand and are essential to rapid scaling. The key is to focus on the most significant behaviors you expect from your sellers. These behaviors should be a main area of focus when hiring. Top-performing salespeople are disciplined and follow a consistent process to create and win opportunities. Even with the SVS architecture to follow, a successful salesperson needs a professional but flexible attitude throughout the sales process. They refine their habits every day through practice and careful attention to detail, leading to success for both them and their companies.

Practicing these habits differentiates your sales team from common sales representatives, which positions you as a trusted advisor. Illustrated in Figure 5.3, these habits—which are inspired by principles found in Stephen Covey's brilliant book *The 7 Habits of Highly Effective People*—will not only benefit you, but your company as well.[6] It's your job to position your company as uniquely qualified to serve the buyer better than your competition.

Seven Habits of Successful Salespeople

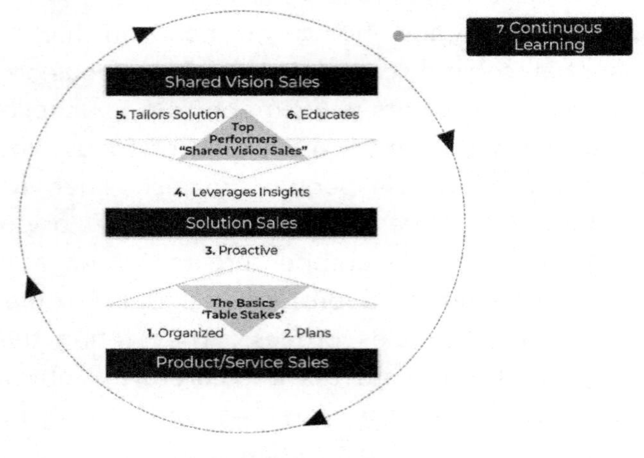

Figure 5.3
(See page 159)

As a salesperson, you want to allocate your time and effort to the highest value opportunities with the highest probability of closing. The key to habits is practicing repetition until routines have formed.

Be Organized

- To keep organized, you need to do your homework or leverage the homework of others. Sharing your plans and documents in a way that others can synchronize with and plan around allows for a unified team. Internal resources are precious but should be easily accessible for everyone involved in the account.

Plan the Work and Work the Plan

- Develop a plan of attack and next step for every qualified opportunity. Updating your approach and next action prepares you to find those "first downs" if a deal is not imminent. By looking ahead, you always have near-term actions to ensure progress.

Be Proactive

- Always be leaning forward to pursue an opportunity rather than sit in "wait and see" mode. Be ready to disqualify or at least de-prioritize marginal opportunities. Practice recognizing when the timing is right or wrong.

Leverage Insights

- Look at the world through the buyer's eyes, and use insight stories and experiences that are relevant to the buyer, not just yourself. When you tell these stories, be mindful of reactions and feedback to correct t he course if necessary.

Tailor Solutions and Differentiate

- One solution does not fit all. While tailoring solutions to buyers, simultaneously promote your company's positive points of differentiation. Understand why your product is unique, but know its limitations as well.

Educate the Buyer

- Add value to every call you make by telling the buyer something they don't already know. Facilitate a higher-quality buying decision, even including "no decision" if necessary. The buyer should be aware of all their options.

Continuously Learn

- Incorporate the art of kaizen, or continuous improvement. Always strive to learn more; there is always another perspective to explore. Make yourself an integral part of the buyer company's differentiated value proposition.

What determines the success rate of these habits is the ability to apply their benefits to situations as they arise. When a problem presents itself, an effective salesperson is already taking the appropriate action to present a solution. By practicing an effective routine throughout your sales process, you'll be able to see your own metrics and output develop over time.

THE IMPORTANCE OF SALES TRAINING

To support a scalable sales process and encourage the right behaviors, top-performing companies leverage sales training. One of the key success factors at the beginning of the scaling process is to take the best practices that were established in the "nail it" phase, document them, and implement an online and facilitated role-based sales training program for all customer-facing professionals in the company. While not everyone in the company will carry a quota or require in-depth sales training, everyone should be able to articulate the company's value proposition and understand the sales process. The highest-performing sales organizations use sales training to build and measure specific sales competencies. The training typically includes sales process training and skill-building modules. Figure 5.4 below displays a sample curriculum and content we developed and delivered for one of our clients.

Figure 5.4

(See page 160)

A tailored, customized sales training program pays for itself through just one or two additional deals. It is one of the lowest-cost, highest-return investments a company can make.

Use the sample criteria below to evaluate your sales maturity. For additional criteria, go to www.salessparx.com.

GTM Maturity Model Analysis: Sales—Model and Process (Sample)

Hiring

- Emerging: The hiring process is solely driven by relationships and past performance.
- Basic: Roles, responsibilities, and metrics are loosely defined, and required behaviors are informally defined.
- Advanced: Roles, responsibilities, metrics, and behaviors are clearly defined and drive the selection of qualified, disciplined candidates.
- Leading: New hires clearly understand their roles, performance expectations, and behavioral requirements. Required skills and knowledge are assessed using formalized testing and case-study-based role play.

Sales Process Consistency

- Emerging: The sales process is undefined with every seller using a unique process.
- Basic: A company-wide sales process exists, and sellers use elements of it during each sale.
- Advanced: A company sales process is well-known with systems in place to ensure sellers are tracking through every phase.
- Leading: The sales process is ubiquitous with recurring sales training and specialized sales enablement tools to ensure adoption and success.

Lead Generation

- **Emerging:** Leads are largely generated opportunistically (from personal contacts or cold calling) with sellers spending time on many unqualified leads.
- Basic: There is an informal lead generation process with a set of recommended qualification criteria. Sellers spend time on less-qualified leads and often utilize other methods of lead generation.
- Advanced: There is a formal lead generation process that all sellers use. Qualification criteria are detailed, and sales resources are only used on well-qualified leads.
- **Leading:** Lead generation and qualification criteria are strictly defined, producing a steady stream of MQLs for sales to follow up on. Once sales resources are brought in, close rates are above 40 percent.

SALESSPARX FUSE CASE STUDY: CARE MANAGEMENT SOFTWARE AND SERVICES COMPANY

A large care management company presented SalesSparx with its $50 million annual sales goal. It was a stretch goal for sure, but it was achievable. When we looked at what it would take to hire a sales team, though, we ran into a problem. It was not cost effective for our client to hire their own team to connect with the thousands of physician practices we needed to secure to meet our stretch goal.

Instead, we offered the care management company another solution: build relationships with organizations that were already calling on hospitals and physician practices. These companies' products would be complementary to the care management company's offerings, creating a more appealing offering. Over the course of a few months, we forged and maintained relationships with these complementary companies, and soon, we had created a sales force of more than 100 people.

With the team assembled, we put together training materials to unify the messaging of those salespeople. Using a shared language to articulate the complementary nature of the care management company's product and its partners, we reached $50 million in sales within less than a year. We could have pushed to build up a sales team with new hires, but leveraging partnerships allowed us to scale at the appropriate rate to reach the stretch goal.

In reality, it was a combination of hiring and partnerships that made this level of growth possible. Though we didn't hire salespeople, we did hire six people to support the 100 salespeople we worked with. By educating this small sales support team about the buyer's journey, we built the right materials and infrastructure to then train the salespeople. The solutions that allow for a flexible and fast approach are never singular. Sometimes, it takes a combination of models to close the deal.

CHAPTER SIX

Sales Maturity—The Revenue Machine

CHAPTER SUMMARY

- A revenue machine is a numeric representation of a company's systematic marketing and sales process to drive consistent, predictable revenue. It can be represented as a sales funnel, where the more you feed to the top of the funnel, the more you can expect to come out on the back end.
- Your existing customers should be a major source of top-of-the-funnel activity, either through referrals or additional areas you can serve them.
- A revenue machine helps companies measure their go-to-market performance, identify bottlenecks, and maintain employee accountability.
- Many companies have informal revenue machines in place, but they don't have a structured format or metrics to monitor their status. Without a formal revenue machine, it can be difficult for a company to identify issues in its sales pipeline, set sales benchmarks, and understand why deals aren't progressing.

All company leaders intuitively understand that they must generate a certain number of meaningful interactions (i.e. sales conversions to generate enough revenue over time). However, SalesSparx finds that many companies need a process for measuring and analyzing these conversions when looking to scale up. This is not to say these companies do not have successful sales processes. The opposite is true, in fact; these informal, ad hoc selling processes do produce some leads and generate enough revenue to maintain the company's operations. The problem emerges when establishing sales benchmarks, identifying areas for process improvement, and ascertaining why deals do not progress. So much opportunity for growth becomes lost when a company does not have clearly defined metrics and forecasting tools.

THE REVENUE MACHINE DEFINED

A properly calibrated revenue machine solves each of these discrepancies and more. As a visual representation of a company's systematic processes, a revenue machine portrays every step of the sales lifecycle to deliver consistent, predictable revenue. A revenue machine can be graphically represented as a sales funnel, as illustrated below. My friend and mentor, Russ Rudish, who retired after leading Deloitte's healthcare and life sciences business, best summed up this concept in the first conversation we had about his sales philosophy: 1) cast a wide net, 2) relentless pursuit, and 3) no excuses. If you apply these simple but powerful concepts to develop and manage your sales funnel, you will be well on your way to success.

Figure 6.1 describes the sales funnel in terms of Rudish's philosophy. The more you feed to the top of the sales funnel, the more you can expect to come out at the bottom. A key input to this funnel should be referrals and new opportunities from existing customers.

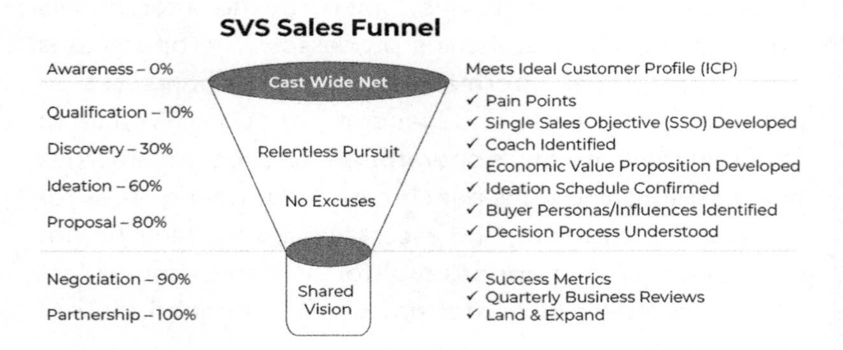

Figure 6.1

(See page 161)

Organizations typically have an informal revenue machine in place, compiling and analyzing some metrics but rarely in a structured and automated format. Maybe they have identified their target market, but they do not have a formal definition of their ideal customer profile or the specific number of organizations that meet their ideal customer profile criteria. Using this unofficial method, leadership continually feels "stuck" with little understanding of how to assess the progress of their awareness efforts.

SalesSparx often hears leaders express, "We've been having conversations with buyers, but we get stuck moving the deal forward." Without a stage-by-stage analysis of their revenue machine's weaknesses, they are not enabled enough to identify the issues within the sales pipeline. In many cases, they do not have a target for how many meaningful interactions they must have to feed the revenue machine. A revenue machine allows leadership to see the sales pipeline as a whole and detect obstructions as well as many other potential roadblocks.

An optimized revenue machine answers the key questions:

- How many target buyers are aware of your brand?
- When they are aware, what did you do to interest them?
- Of those interested, how many qualify with your ideal profile criteria?
- Of those qualified, how many proceed to each SVS sales stage?
- Where are we getting stuck?

The revenue machine documents the progress of deals within the SVS process, whether they are in qualification, discovery, ideation, or another stage, and allows you to predict how those deals will result based on probabilities. For example, an organization could qualify many deals, yet these deals do not move to the discovery stage. Knowing this information, the organization is better equipped to change its messaging or sales process. When you understand how a revenue machine functions, you understand your organization's strengths and weaknesses. When you understand your organization's strengths and weaknesses, you understand how to grow.

A revenue machine also helps maintain employee accountability. For example, a company may hire a salesperson and provide them with training. After six months, if that salesperson has not met their quota, the company may elect to terminate their employment. With a revenue machine in place, though, the company may see the salesperson has conducted 10 meaningful interactions with buyers and has several deals in the early stages of the sales process. The salesperson has performed well, but without the ability to measure their sales pipeline status, the company executives cannot clearly see their skill level.

The key to leadership making a proper diagnosis is to blame the process, not the people. Salespeople don't join a team only to intentionally neglect their duties and perform poorly. In my experience, there is typically an underlying issue either prohibiting their competency or masking how much they are truly achieving. Perhaps the product's differentiation is not sufficiently highlighted, or maybe the process for sharing best practices could be better optimized. A revenue machine provides a replicable, measurable process for gathering data, determining these barriers, and brainstorming how to address them in the most beneficial way possible.

Figure 6.2 is an example of a revenue machine report that is ideally generated by your CRM.

Revenue Machine Report - Sample

Sales Process	Unique Web Visits/ Month	MQLs* /Visits	MQLs/ Month	SQL/ MQL	Web Based SQLs/ Month	Decision-Maker Meetings / Month	SQL/ Meetings	SQLs/ Year	Win Rate	Wins	Average Deal Size (ARR)	Contracted ARR
Current Revenue Machine	100	0	0	0	0	8	5%	48	35%	17	$350,000	~$6M
With SalesSparx FUSE	2,000	1%	20	10%	2	100	10%	96	35%	34	$400,000	$13.6M
With SalesSparx FUSE (Stretch)*	**5,000**	**2%**	**100**	**20%**	**20**	**100**	**15%**	**168**	**40%**	**67**	**$500,000**	**$33.5M**

*MQL – Marketing Qualified Lead, SQL – Sales Qualified Lead, ARR – Annualized Recurring Revenue

Figure 6.2
(See page 162)

Whether you have a non-recurring or recurring revenue model, a revenue machine answers the question: how will you convert your deals into revenue? If you have an optimized revenue machine, you may see that 40 percent of deals within the ideation stage end up closing. With 10 deals in ideation, you can feel confident that you will close four of those within your average sales cycle.

To ensure that your customer receives optimal customer service and your delivery team does not become overwhelmed, you must take action by hiring a new delivery specialist, increasing employee productivity in the department, or finding a way to manage incoming projects. This example reveals how a honed revenue machine allows for alignment between marketing, sales, and delivery—an essential collaboration that decreases the likelihood of obstacles within the sales process and allows leaders to identify, measure, and tackle discrepancies in a holistic manner.

For recurring revenue companies, such as healthcare SaaS companies, the revenue machine should include your unit economics. It is critical to measure metrics such as your customer acquisition costs (CAC), gross margins, lifetime value (LTV), and payback period. These drivers will be the first pieces of information a private equity or venture capital company will want to understand if you seek outside investment.

Cross-functional adoption of the company revenue machine rewards organizations with massive growth. Founders who do not micromanage and instead allow their employees to take ownership over revenue machine metrics and execute plans surrounding that data see truly sustainable success.

Use the sample criteria below to evaluate your revenue machine maturity. For additional criteria, go to www.salessparx.com.

GTM Maturity Model Analysis: Sales—The Revenue Machine

Marketing Metrics

- Emerging: The company does not capture or analyze metrics to optimize the marketing process.
- Basic: Key metrics are defined, but captured data is inconsistent or not fully utilized.
- Advanced: Key metrics are systematically captured and analyzed with insights being provided to sellers.
- Leading: The importance of key metrics is understood by every marketer, and they are all aware of their numbers. Insights from the data are utilized to create useful sales enablement tools and training content.

Sales Metrics

- Emerging: The company does not capture or analyze metrics to optimize its sales process.
- Basic: Key metrics are defined, but data capture is inconsistent or not fully utilized.
- Advanced: Key metrics are systematically captured and analyzed with insights being provided to sellers.
- Leading: The importance of key metrics is understood by every seller, and they are all aware of their numbers. Insights from the data are utilized to create useful sales enablement tools and training content.

Unit Economics

- Emerging: The company has a conceptual understanding of its unit economic drivers but is not measuring performance.
- Basic: The company roughly tracks customer acquisition cost, lifetime value, unit gross margins, and other key unit economic measures.
- Advanced: The company tracks and manages its unit economic metrics as part of its financial reporting processes.
- Leading: The company manages its unit economics and has achieved industry-leading metrics in areas such as payback period, customer acquisition cost (CAC), and lifetime value (LTV).

SALESSPARX FUSE CASE STUDY: HEALTHCARE IT CONSULTING COMPANY

As discussed in Chapter One, a great team and I once built a highly successful management consulting division within an IT staffing company using the strategies detailed in this book. While the FUSE methodology catalyzed our success, my team and I could have never achieved such results without the use of an advanced revenue machine.

Revenue generation served as one of our primary objectives, and as such, we set extremely aggressive targets, aiming to reach $10 million in revenue by the end of year one. To set appropriate and achievable goals for reaching this amount, we first had to answer key questions:

- What will be the size of our average deal?
- How long will it take to sell each deal?
- How many conversations must we have to produce enough MQLs?
- How many MQLs will proceed to the discovery stage?

What numbers do we need to hit and maintain in order to reach our annual revenue goal?

We first set a revenue goal and then worked our way backward through the SVS process to ensure we had enough opportunities at each stage. Plotting these components into a revenue machine guaranteed we made enough investments in the front end to produce enough awareness and then move deals forward. For example, 12 sales representatives sold staffing solutions offerings that significantly differed from the strategic solutions my team sold. Though they did not have the knowledge or training to sell our consulting services, we did educate them on the buyer pain points to look for and create incentives for them, encouraging them to introduce our offerings to their prospective buyers and open doors for us along the way. Then, once they opened the doors, our team moved in to complete the sales process, a system that leveraged existing relationships to empower the division's rapid growth. The revenue machine not only allowed us to set these incentives and growth objectives, but it also revealed how the process worked to increase total sales, contributing to the $0 to $60 million increase in revenue over a three-year period.

CHAPTER SEVEN

Delivery Maturity

CHAPTER SUMMARY

- A clear understanding of the delivery process is crucial during the sales process to ensure customer satisfaction and trust in the company.
- Sales engineers or the delivery team should be consulted as early as the ideation phase of the SVS sales process to provide a clear, mappable path between what the buyer needs and the offered solutions.
- It is crucial to understand the cost of delivery and the importance of setting criteria for scaling up, such as team training effectiveness, customer satisfaction scores, and measurements of delivered value.
- Organizations should track delivery profitability not only through financial reports, but also by measuring the amount of time the delivery team spends on each project.
- Account management should develop into account expansion, allowing for multiple opportunities to come from a single account.

Buyers have certain expectations, especially if they have been given guarantees by a salesperson. If the offering does not deliver as expected, they may feel the salesperson over-promised and under-delivered. It may even seem as if they have been intentionally misled. More likely than not, the sales team and customer encountered a misunderstanding, or the offering had limitations that the sales team was unaware of. This is a common enough problem that a joke has risen out of it:

"What's the difference between a solution salesperson and a used car salesperson?"

"The solution salesperson didn't know when they were wrong."

Proper delivery requires a sales team that is well-trained in the offering and all its associated moving parts. To effectively scale up, the path between what the buyer needs and the provided solutions should be easily mappable and clear for both the seller and the buyer. This path may not be intrinsically evident to a salesperson, so sales engineers or the delivery team should be consulted earlier in the customer journey. Following the SVS model, delivery should be addressed around the ideation stage, well before a proposal has been agreed upon. During ideation, the seller and buyer establish mutual trust, which requires providing the buyer with a clear understanding of the delivery process.

Including a member of the delivery team during the ideation stage brings a level of expertise and cements your organization's credibility in the eye of the buyer. If they understand your offering and how it will integrate into their own systems, it will hold more value as they build a sense of ownership around the potential new systems. The key is not to waste the delivery team's time; by pulling them away for sales meetings, they have less time to do their own jobs. If a deal is entering the ideation stage, it has already been qualified; it should be worth the team's time to help clinch the sale. As the buyer adopts the shared vision, the technical aspects allow them to visualize workflow and technology integration and the potential of their new system. It also enables them to educate their own internal teams as to how necessary your product is. Some organizations can emphasize delivery optimization in the sales process with sales engineers. A salesperson can only know so much about the product before the more technical details escape their knowledge base. By collaborating on a potential sale, salespeople and sales engineers can ensure that the handoff to delivery will be as smooth as possible.

THE COST OF DELIVERY

Every organization is different, but no matter the company's focus or organizational structure, delivery measurement criteria need to be in place. These quantifiable benchmarks include team training effectiveness, customer satisfaction scores, and measurements of delivered value. Were you able to deliver what you said you would? Are you able to replicate this repeatedly? How much did it cost to deliver your offering?

Initially, you may not meet those success criteria, particularly when determining the cost of delivery. Over time, you want to be able to reduce the cost of implementation for your business, understanding the unit economics. Many organizations we've worked with do not have the necessary metrics in place to calculate accurate unit economics and remain unaware of the cost to acquire a new customer. Initially integrating your offering into the buyer's structure may eat into revenue, especially with recurring revenue models, but as customers continue to do business with you, the acquisition cost will eventually be paid for, following the "land and expand" model.

Most organizations track profitability solely through the lens of a financial report, measuring revenue against expenses. The amount of time your delivery team spends on each project may not be easily reflected in dollars, but it holds a great amount of value. If the initial implementation takes your team an extended period of time, it may not be profitable to search out only new sales opportunities. The "one and done" methodology limits your product lifecycle and profitability; it should continue to bring new value to your customer.

LAND AND EXPAND

With success criteria in place, every buyer's needs will be measured at different levels. Your opportunities as a company are in those gaps between what the buyer is doing and what they need to be successful. Figure 7.1 below highlights the various conversations and activities required to help customers transition from where they are today to where they want to be.

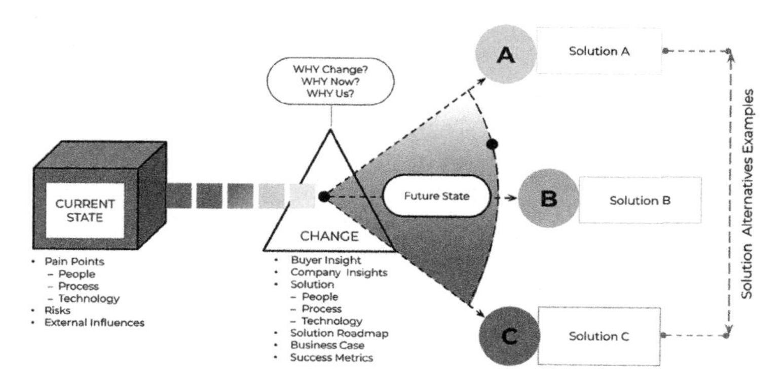

Figure 7.1

(See page 163)

By identifying these blind spots, you can expand the service you provide, adding more functionality to your products and service. Those success criteria should be agreed upon by the buyer, though; their success is your success.

The hardest part of selling is generally not the actual design of a solution—it's the cultivation of buyer trust and confidence. "One and done" sales techniques require finding new leads, spending time to raise awareness, qualifying these potential buyers, and then selling to them—a lot of effort for little return. When you can land and expand a business relationship, the relationship is already there. You've essentially fast-tracked awareness, qualification, and discovery and can go right into ideation with new solutions to their blind spots.

As this business relationship matures, it gives you the opportunity to begin listening and understanding your buyer. Once your product has been implemented into a customer's system, the voice of the customer should be documented and distributed in a cross-functional effort between team members. This feedback is invaluable. It's not uncommon for customers to realize new wants and needs for expanded solutions as they roll out and start to scale. If their feedback provides additional functionality across your solution lifecycle, that's added value to all other customers.

ENSURING CUSTOMER SUCCESS

The feedback gathered during the delivery process should be formalized for a data-driven approach to trend and pattern recognition. Every time a customer struggles after solution implementation, value is lost, and your relationship may be tarnished. There may be some initial quick wins when your product is first implemented, but unless the customer journey continues with enthusiasm and exploration, you risk the relationship.

This decline in customer satisfaction, especially for software, can often be a direct result of a poor understanding of the product's capabilities. Unless the customer's organization has an executive sponsor and superusers who know how to use the solution and drive it forward, customer success may not be realized. It has become increasingly common to see user certification programs offered alongside software products. These programs ensure that the customer's organization understands the capabilities of either the technology or service being offered. Sometimes, if a company becomes certified in a software, it reduces its support fees, incentivizing the buyer organization to make sure their teams properly utilize the solution. The added value only compounds if you can land and expand your relationship with the customer. With the user certification program, customers will be able to communicate their feedback with greater specificity as they know your product in and out. How that feedback is captured determines how useful it is.

Information flow must be cross-functional between teams, specifically between delivery teams and account executives. Account managers generally report back to sales while delivery teams have their own separate insights from implementation. The union of these two avenues creates a more complete picture of the customer's journey. A partnership between your heads of delivery and account management leads to delivery becoming a well-oiled machine, replicating success with every implementation.

ACCOUNT MANAGEMENT

SalesSparx often comes across companies with no account management process in place: there's no formal plan to follow up with customers once the initial delivery is done. Follow up is simply an action item that people mean to complete but rarely do. That initial sale should not be the end goal, but rather the beginning of an expanded relationship that starts to pay returns. Existing business and contacts are some of the most valuable assets you can have; they are the foundation of land and expand. This is where account planning becomes critical to synchronize your company with the needs of your customers.

Account expansion isn't possible if your delivery or sales teams move on after landing. For some organizations, the salesperson who landed the account will stay on to manage it. This system benefits smaller companies as the salesperson can maintain that continuous relationship. If you're large enough, you'll have one team solely focused on new sales and another on management. Figure 7.2 shows a sample of an integrated sales and account management process and associated key metrics.

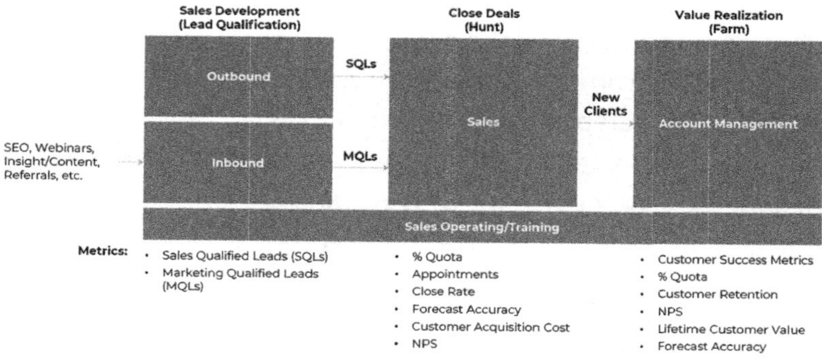

Figure 7.2

(See page 164)

While your sales team focuses on "hunting" for new deals, account managers can keep "farming" the customers you already have. To scale up to this level, your organization will have to consider the complexity of your offering. A less complex offering can be handed off to the delivery team with fewer consequences, compared to a complex offering that needs custom parameters and a steady hand through management.

By managing scope, cost, and time across your delivery methodology, you can ensure a higher quality in offering while maintaining flexibility across the delivery process. As every customer has different needs, adjusting your budget, functionality, and schedule can keep the necessary level of quality to continue helping them reach success. If your customer has a very strict deadline to meet and you need to accelerate the delivery process, features may be reduced, and costs may be raised to fit that timeline.

Account managers should be able to understand the customer's current state, how your product will help them redesign the transformation process, and how to monitor all outcomes. Your team will help them adapt to the change and integrate the software as they go. The goal is to propel customers to the desired levels of success while maintaining clearly defined objectives. Key activities, responsibilities, and deliverables will vary depending on organizations, customer bases, and offerings, but the delivery process should be tracked all the same.

When delivery teams and account managers are prepared for projects coming down the sales pipeline, they can bring value to the customer as soon as the deal is signed. That degree of attention builds the necessary relationship to continue along the land and expand methodology. By having a unified, cross-functional effort monitoring all the necessary data through the delivery process, customers will see the benefits of your offering and the future potential that comes with it.

Use the sample criteria below to evaluate your delivery maturity. For additional criteria, go to www.salessparx.com.

GTM Maturity Model Analysis: Delivery (Sample)

Sales-Delivery Handoff

- Emerging: Delivery and sales have very limited communication with delivery details only touched upon in the sales process.
- Basic: Informal communication occurs between sales and delivery, mostly around timing and a few key points of service.

- Advanced: Formal communication occurs between sales and delivery with sales actively capturing key delivery information and providing a structured handoff post-sale.
- Leading: Resources of delivery are integrated into the sales process to generate increased buyer commitment to the solution. Delivery and sales actively communicate to ensure a smooth handoff as the sale is closing.

Account Development

- Emerging: Every sale is a one-off with no long-term strategies for account development.
- Basic: Simple account management is in place to check in with buyers if they express a need for further solutions.
- Advanced: Robust account management is in place that tracks buyer engagement and collects data that can be used to start future opportunities.
- Leading: Success metrics are well-defined, and quarterly business reviews and other regular meetings are conducted to measure progress. New opportunities are regularly identified to address customer pain points.

Replicable Methodology

- Emerging: The offering methodology is unique to each customer.
- Basic: A standard offering has crystallized with repeatable methodologies.

- Advanced: A replicable methodology is defined to extend a core interoperability offering.
- Leading: A replicable methodology is proven to provide clients with expected results.

SALESSPARX FUSE CASE STUDY: HEALTHCARE CLOUD ENABLEMENT COMPANY

Working with a healthcare cloud company that enables healthcare organizations to move from local data centers to the cloud, my team and I found that every buyer falls on a different place along a cloud and security maturity scale and requires different assistance when executing these transformations. For example, some organizations had outstanding IT security, but they did not have a clear grasp on cloud integration and vice versa. With a blanket delivery process, customers struggled to adopt their systems in a productive way. The key to elevating the IT security company's delivery was to help them meet the customer where they were; the company required a standardized methodology for gauging an organization's security and cloud capability levels.

Customers should feel like they are always moving in the right direction along the buyer's journey with success very clearly marked. We helped the IT security company build a capability model to assess each customer's capabilities and then prescribe the appropriate level of services to guide them along the journey and meet their individual objectives. With every customer in a different position on the spectrum, offerings could be systematically adjusted to their needs, which included packaging enough support and training for those struggling to close their capability gaps.

We find organizations are sometimes hesitant to package additional services in their offerings. However, if you don't, your customers will struggle to extract the full value from your product. Without the full benefits of your offering, you will feel strain in the buyer and seller relationship, dampening any opportunities to land and expand. A happy, healthy customer base is necessary to scale at an accelerated rate. As the IT security company raised its customer satisfaction, its close rates went up, along with its ability to upsell.

CHAPTER EIGHT

Enablement Technology Maturity

CHAPTER SUMMARY

- Automation technology can ease challenges by instituting clear milestones and process steps for employees to adopt the same language and best practices. Automation tools also help increase productivity, reduce the potential for human error, and improve process compliance, which are essential for scaling up a business.
- Two categories of technology are most impactful for company growth: sales automation and marketing automation.

Organizations across all industries struggle to find and implement the appropriate software and technologies to automate their marketing and sales efforts. In addition to discovering and analyzing information surrounding new technologies, leadership must also understand the value of the technology, allocate funds to purchase it, integrate it into the established system, and train their employees in adoption. When company leaders concern themselves with a constant assortment of daily hurdles, researching new automation practices is often not the highest priority. Every minute of their day is valuable, so even if a technology could increase productivity, many do not have the initial time or expenses to invest.

Many leaders believe they do not have the time or resources to invest in researching new technologies and understanding their value, which can lead to a lack of adoption. Instead, employees often rely on manual processes, creating their own personal methods rather than using standardized company practices. Though most leaders recognize how more automation could streamline processes and increase overall effectiveness, they are so accustomed to pounding the pavement themselves that they do not gain awareness of what technology exists and how it can help. A lack of bandwidth can cause leaders to focus on day-to-day tasks rather than future objectives, and it is sometimes difficult to recognize how automation can benefit a company in the long run. This is especially true when the technology can take a fair amount of time to produce substantial effects. As a result, the inertia is often not present to complete all the necessary integration steps efficiently, especially if leadership does not recognize how the software can improve operations.

SalesSparx most often sees companies with minimal levels of automation. Employees manually make phone calls and update spreadsheets, creating their own personal processes rather than using a standardized methodology built by the company. Automation technology combats this discrepancy, instituting clear milestones and process steps for employees to adopt the same language and best practices. Through monitoring mechanisms, you can set reminders for employees to complete certain tasks by a specified date and time, or you can establish step-by-step checklists to guide employees through entire processes. In addition to key company components, such as a revenue machine or account management function, proper technology usage also enables you to identify where deals become stuck and how to best move forward. Once you understand *what* to measure, your IT analytics should enable you to measure it and identify gaps in the resulting metrics, allowing you to see where you are today versus where you want to be in the future.

Figure 8.1 below is a sample of the minimum information you need to automate and measure.

Figure 8.1
(See page 165)

AUTOMATION TOOLS AND THEIR USES

Maximizing technological capabilities empowers companies to scale more quickly. Manually sending emails, for example, is not cost effective. If you wish to send 400 marketing emails, you will find greater, more sustainable success by setting up an automated marketing tool than you would assigning the task to an individual. In addition, an automated marketing tool will send you routine reports over those emails, detailing factors such as how many buyers opened the emails and how many clicked on a link within the text.

In contrast, paying an individual to complete the same task not only costs more immediate money, but also reduces the time an employee must complete more important projects. This extra work, in addition to the decrease in project turnover rate, impacts overall revenue in ways that can be easy to miss, especially without the correct revenue machine or metric-monitoring system in place. Process compliance also improves alongside productivity as automation tools decrease the potential for human error. Tracking necessary data and information by hand limits company growth in each of these ways, making technological automation the backbone of scalable organizations.

Two categories of technology pertain to this book: sales automation and marketing automation.

Sales technology generally relates to CRM automation, which centers around capturing information about the buyer or customer so you may serve them better, whether the customer is an existing pursuit or not. With both sales and marketing technology, a problem occurs when businesses attempt to introduce the technology before the fundamental aspects of their company's structure. For example, a CRM cannot be effectively implemented without the company utilizing a standardized sales process. SalesSparx often sees companies purchase industry-leading CRM software without a structural understanding of what they are trying to accomplish with it.

Marketing technology automates the function of awareness, meaning it increases the number of buyers who are aware of your brand and further encourages them to make a purchase. Many companies will invest in the technology, yet they do not invest enough in the foundational content and branding component. If a message does not currently resonate in the market, promoting it on a larger scale via marketing automation will not boost awareness or sales. "Spraying and praying" your message will not achieve desired results. Rather, you must ask yourself: how do you promote content that is relevant to your specific audience? If you primarily sell to

CFO audiences, then CFOs will require a certain type of information to pique their interest. In contrast, a COO will desire an entirely different set of information. Integrating marketing automation still requires the users to consider their ideal personas, and while technology can certainly help you achieve this, a human touch is required to make marketing initiatives truly successful.

Examples of marketing automation tools include lead management software, content delivery systems, and content management technologies. Sales automation tools, in comparison, include process management software, proposal resources, and presentation developers. Though SalesSparx most often guides organizations through CRM development, we have identified several essential technologies for companies to consider implementing. As you read through each category, note that you will need to consider several factors when choosing the right technology for your company:

- Does the technology adhere to your budget?
- Is the technology scalable?
- Does the technology offer the features you need to be successful?
- Does the technology align with your established sales process?
- Will the technology be simple to use, or will it require more in-depth training?

Content Delivery and Management Technology

Content delivery and management tools are used to automate recurring marketing activities. As with any software, every tool offers a diverse set of options and features, including email campaigns, drip sequences, CRM functionality, lead scoring, text messaging, and more. These tools enable you to save time and reduce the manpower needed to launch widespread marketing initiatives. In addition, they also allow you to generate more conclusive, specific data and institute personalized marketing campaigns, which then lead to increased conversion rates and more brand awareness.

Lead Generation Software

Searching and contacting potential leads consumes much of a salesperson's time if not automated. Lead generation software aims not only to generate more leads with less work on the salesperson's end, but also to bring in higher-quality leads that better match your ideal audience. Most software achieves this by compiling a list of potential leads and their contact information from online sources, such as social media, email campaigns, and websites. Based on the data the software pulls, you can then create more targeted marketing strategies, which results in increased brand awareness, more MQLs, and more profitable deals.

Customer Relationship Management (CRM) Software

Competing in any industry now requires the use of a CRM, one of the most critical applications a company can utilize. A CRM is a tool that enables companies to access, organize, and analyze customer data. This resource acts as a one-stop shop for compiling notes, activities, and metrics into one cohesive system so that cross-departmental functions can access the same customer information, allowing for better coordination and increased customer satisfaction. Organizations can also use these tools to create customized reports to improve forecast accuracy, manage their revenue machine, and analyze overall pipeline performance. CRMs are designed to be scalable, meaning all companies, no matter their size, can utilize and grow with the CRM of their choice.

Learning Management Systems (LMSs)

Learning Management Systems (LMSs) also act as key components that train team members in product knowledge, sales process, sales skills, and more. If you are an organization that heavily values learning, you can align your LMS with your determined sales competencies, building software that coaches salespeople in:

- what they must know about the product,
- what they must know to be a successful sales representative, and
- what sales techniques have proved the most useful.

Conversation Intelligence (CI) Tools

Conversation Intelligence (CI) tools allow you to capture the conversations between your sales team and customers. The software records, transcribes, and even analyzes sales calls, identifying the most-used keywords and allowing salespeople to see areas of improvement. This type of technology can be used to determine non-compliant topics of conversation, identify ineffective sales tactics, and train new sales representatives on best practices.

BEST PRACTICES FOR IMPLEMENTING AUTOMATION

SalesSparx encounters four prominent scenarios when ascertaining a company's need for technology. The company either struggles with:

Lack of technology

- The company operates with little to no technology, carrying out each necessary process in a manual fashion. The leadership either does not have the bandwidth to research, review, purchase, and integrate technology, or leaders do not see how a new technology could improve their operations in both the long and short term.

Lack of best practices

- Maybe a company does use a technology, but the tool is not being correctly applied by all or most of the employees. A lack of technical training then leads to a lack of company-wide adoption.

Lack of adoption

- As the technology has never been properly explained, employees fail to use it correctly, or the technology seems so inaccessible and frustrating that no one uses it altogether.

Lack of standardization

- Individuals within the company use different technologies to accomplish the same tasks, which leads to ineffective communication and resource sharing.

Company leadership can contest these roadblocks by acknowledging three basic considerations:

1. **Education**
   a. Employees must understand the technology to wield it effectively. Team members will not employ the technology, no matter how useful, if they cannot navigate it.
   b. An LMS can be a useful resource for ensuring every individual learns and can reproduce specific skills, though any sort of concentrated training effort or resource is better than no effort at all.
2. **Adoption**
   a. Once employees understand the technology, the tool must be ingrained in their daily processes and enforced. The technology should be used to create required materials, such as reports and presentations.
3. **Leadership**
   a. One person should hold responsibility for monitoring the progress of sales and marketing automation, recognizing how to better

facilitate technological adoption and understanding how the technology is being used across the organization.

Leadership acts as the foundation for each of these considerations. The leadership team must clearly understand both long-term and short-term company objectives and what pieces need to be introduced to meet those goals. Whether you have gaps in the right people, right culture, right process, or right technology, everything comes together when each component works together. Leadership must have the ability to determine improvement areas, push agendas forward, and execute on these components to allow the company to reach its fullest potential. The team should ensure employees receive the necessary education and enforce technological adoption at all levels so that progress can occur.

Similarly, the leadership team must also have a company-wide sales process in place before introducing a technology. No amount of software will ever help you if you do not have an established process to use alongside it. Remember, technology is not the answer; technology helps you execute the answer. Technology *can* influence your process as your organization evolves, though. Certain technological capabilities may provide you with new tools and methods for completing tasks that were not previously possible. However, if you do not have a solid process established from the beginning, then technology will only help you automate inefficiency. You will only achieve incompetency faster.

As automation tools continue to evolve, they will always point to the fundamentals of sales and marketing, including the need for a well-established sales process and leadership. These automation tools, no matter how advanced, help us gather and interpret basic information: customer needs, how we can help the customer meet those needs, and how we can better adapt our organizations to improve our operations. For example, data mining has recently been a popular sales practice. If a business leader searches the keyword "CRM" on Google, then a CRM company may be informed of this search and show them an increased volume of CRM advertisements. I only see this, alongside other automation practices, becoming more and more prominent. These new innovations and tactics do not change the tasks we must accomplish to scale sustainably, though; they change—and may revolutionize—the way we carry out those tasks.

Use the sample criteria below to evaluate your enablement technology maturity. For additional criteria, go to www.salessparx.com.

GTM Maturity Model Analysis: Enablement Technology (Sample)

Marketing Automation

- Emerging: The company does not use any sales or marketing automation.
- Basic: Leadership has invested in sales and marketing automation, but only basic functionality is utilized due to a lack of training and understanding of benefits.
- Advanced: The company leverages sales and marketing technology to streamline lead generation with standards in place to ensure utilization.

- Leading: Marketing technology is made accessible through customized training and frequent demonstration. They produce high-quality leads and data to guide leadership decisions.

Leadership Buy-In

- Emerging: Leadership does not oversee technology education, adoption, or management.
- Basic: Leadership recognizes the need for technological education and adoption and advises management on best practices.
- Advanced: Leadership oversees education, adoption, and management of technology, providing formal resources for sellers to utilize.
- Leading: Leadership oversees education, adoption, and management of technology, crafting utilization strategies that maximize the effectiveness of technology investments.

Sales Automation

- Emerging: Each seller manages their own accounts, leveraging the technologies and strategies that they prefer.
- Basic: Sellers follow a standardized account management process on a CRM, but utilization is low and little data is captured.
- Advanced: CRM utilization is mandatory with sellers documenting sales data as deals progress. Training is provided to ensure adoption.

- Leading: The company has a CRM customized to their sales needs, tracking key sales metrics and providing leadership with detailed insight into the sales pipeline.

SALESSPARX FUSE CASE STUDY: DATA ANALYTICS COMPANY

When SalesSparx first began working with a data analytics company, we immediately recognized that the organization did not define which prospects were an ideal fit for its offerings. We helped them determine their ideal customer profile, creating a comprehensive list of applicable US health systems and the points of contact within those organizations. Using marketing automation, we then disseminated thought leadership content targeted at their ideal customer profile and personas. This built more brand awareness, which created additional leads across the organization.

At the time of SalesSparx's introduction, the data analytics company had the free version of a CRM but did not use it. Rather than purchase and integrate a CRM from day one, we implemented SVS. Using an LMS, SalesSparx coached employees through each stage of SVS as well as fundamental skills, such as conducting executive conversations and handling objections. The SVS "app" was then loaded onto the CRM to quickly automate the SVS process. This pre-loaded approach potentially saved the company more than $100,000 as it could simply take the existing process and drop it into a CRM instead of building a process from scratch. This new system led to faster lead identification, better close rates, a more predictable sales process, and more reliable forecasting.

THE SALESSPARX FUSE™ IMPLEMENTATION PLAYBOOK

One of my Stanford professors, Dr. Robert Sutton, wrote a great book called *The Knowing-Doing Gap: How Smart Companies Turn Knowledge into Action*. The idea is that most people know (or can learn) what to do but don't do it. One of the reasons is the lack of a clear action plan.[7] Here is a roadmap for pulling your FUSE GTM plan together. Note that steps one through five can and should ideally be completed in 45 days or less.

Step 1: Rate the GTM maturity of each FUSE GTM component.

We have documented dozens of best practices for each FUSE component depending on whether you offer software, technology, services, or a combination. At the end of Chapters Two through Seven, we have a list of evaluation criteria you can use to get started. If you need additional criteria, go to www.salessparx.com.

Step 2: Determine the key decisions you need to make to go from where you are today to the next level.

If you rate a GTM component as Emerging or Basic, what actions can you take to move to the next level? Some of the essential decisions include:

- What is our stretch goal?
- What are our Three Whys?

- How do we organize our sales team to drive better performance?
- Is there a better way to articulate and quantify our value to buyers?
- How do we overcome common objections to our offerings?
- Is there a way to better align our marketing and sales teams?
- What is our revenue machine?
- How do we improve the way we gather and act on customer feedback?

Step 3: Schedule a one-and-a-half-day FUSE GTM kickoff meeting to review the ratings with your leadership team, make the key GTM decisions, and develop the first draft of your FUSE GTM plan.

Prior to the kickoff session, schedule a meeting to share the gap analysis and key decisions with the attendees. Gather their input on these areas, and ask them to document their view of the company's GTM SWOT analysis and send it to you. Organize their input into a preliminary SWOT.

Step 4: Conduct the meeting using the following agenda:

Day 1 (full day):

- Review and finalize the GTM SWOT.
- Review the key gaps, and make GTM decisions.
- Determine GTM execution risks and mitigation strategies.

Day 2 (½ day):

Using the SWOT and GTM decisions as input, develop a FUSE GTM plan for the next 6–12 months. This will be FUSE GTM 1.0.

- Develop FUSE GTM objectives and key results (OKRs).
- Develop a FUSE GTM action plan to support the achievement of the OKRs.
- Create a FUSE GTM risk mitigation plan.
- Schedule a meeting for the following week to finalize the FUSE GTM plan.

Step 5: Review the FUSE GTM draft, and finalize it.

Document the GTM OKRs and actions in a project management tool where you can assign accountability and deadlines.

Step 6: Schedule and conduct two 45-minute, weekly meetings to examine progress and address any GTM risks or issues.

Step 7: Implement the SVS process, and automate it using a CRM.

Step 8: Repeat steps one through five every 6–12 months, ensuring you limit GTM refresh meetings to half-day timeslots.

As you move from FUSE GTM 1.0 to 2.0 and beyond, continue to rate your maturity. This improved maturity will result in improved sales performance.

If you are like our typical clients and follow this playbook step by step, you should see a sales increase of 20 percent to 100 percent. If you have questions or would like a sample FUSE GTM report, do not hesitate to contact us at www.salessparx.com.

CONCLUSION

Healthcare is the most complex industry to sell into as every facet concerns the human condition. All work boils down to a matter of life or death, even when the stakes may seem small and manageable. Mistakes in healthcare have severe implications: kids grow up without parents, grandparents are gone too soon, a spouse is lost forever. Healthcare organizations strive to impact complex problems that require innovative solutions, and improving their workflows means ensuring that a new drug is developed faster, or patients are more efficiently cared for. In other words, the way you sell to people dealing with this stress vastly differs from other industries. My hope is that this book emphasizes the unique nature of the healthcare industry and also demonstrates the true objective of sales in general: to focus on your prospective buyer's needs and help them reach their goals.

By pursuing this objective, your customer's goals will enact the industry change needed for system-wide transformation. When many people think about healthcare, they focus on sickness as a problem that needs to be solved, but in truth, the real answers lie in promoting health. The current system incentivizes only helping individuals when they are sick rather than cultivating their continued well-being. These healthcare practices, as they stand, are unsustainable and contain gaps worth filling, which were made even more apparent by the global COVID-19 pandemic. Patients are not the only ones suffering: physicians feel more burnt out and undervalued than ever. SalesSparx wants to make strides in tackling these issues, helping companies reduce their costs, improving their focus on health, and achieving improved sales performance and revenue generation. The longer collaboration and innovation in healthcare stalls, the longer we continue to lose lives and money in the process. We know that helping you bring your innovations to market, with a replicable and proven approach, is what it will take to see the industry change for the better.

Progress requires approaching change with a spirit of curiosity. What could your organization do differently? What could your organization do better? Enacting large-scale change requires bravery: bravery to realize established plans are not working, bravery to realize your own limitations as a leader, and bravery to try new tactics openly. Leaders who have maintained a high-level position at a company for decades may struggle to consider new structures, processes, and ideas, but at the end of the day, these leaders must evolve alongside their companies, even if some transitions are not easy to accept. If your organization is not currently performing at the highest level possible, work from curiosity, unite your team around a shared vision, and make the growth happen.

My time with management consulting firms and software companies showed me the range of solutions that businesses can initiate, given the right tools and resources. It's unfortunate to see some solutions lost to time as the businesses did not achieve their true growth potential. The SalesSparx team and I want to make sure that innovation no longer slips through the cracks; by inspiring leadership in organizations to take stock of their teams and capabilities, we can help them hold onto the solutions that have the ability to change the world. By maintaining the FUSE process, developing a FUSE GTM plan, and tapping into the potential of SVS, you have a proven roadmap that will raise these chances of success.

Outlining the FUSE process provided you with the tools. Now, it is your responsibility to apply them. No book, no matter how thorough, can optimize your business for you. All organizations differ, and a universal, one-size-fits-all strategy does not exist. The key is for executives to adopt the FUSE process, employ SVS, and analyze their company from the lens of a GTM maturity scale. Some organizations may have the resources to carry this out themselves with moderate coaching while others may work together with outside assistance to reach their objectives. Along the same lines, other companies may hire a third party to carry out their scaling initiatives from start to finish for them. Whichever approach you choose, the principles described in this book build upon your company's already established foundation and your current long-term business plan to build a customized GTM plan for exceeding your sales and marketing revenue targets. Begin acting on these ideas today, and this book will empower your company to provide better care for patients on a larger, more sustainable scale, potentially transforming health.

If you're in healthcare, you're making a difference. While helpful, standard business advice does exist across all industries, I hope this book provides you with versatile sales and marketing information that you can use to succeed within a healthcare setting. Reading the final pages of this book, you should feel better equipped to perform a practical SWOT analysis, identify the more significant gaps in your existing go-to-market strategy, and devise an actionable GTM plan for reaching your stretch goal and surpassing your growth objectives.

If you still find you need an extra resource, do not hesitate to reach out to us for more assistance. The SalesSparx team always feels privileged at the opportunity to help spur healthcare innovation in any capacity.

ACKNOWLEDGMENTS

I am humbled by the talented clients we work with. Each company has different areas of focus on its path to improved go-to-market maturity, yet they all have a common passion to make healthcare better. We learned from them as much as they learned from us.

I could not have done this without the talent and support of Alexander Gomez. His insights, research, writing skills, and problem solving kept me moving forward, even when it got really hard.

Also, much thanks to Mike Sweeney, Russ Rudish, Dr. Mitch Morris, Scott Kolesar, Dave Vreeland, Anthony McCarley, Arvind Kumar, Dr. Ramin Rafiei, Mark Rangell, Alli Luchey, and Simon Gisby who went through all 132 pages to provide amazing ideas about how better to present FUSE and our ideas.

Last but not least, much thanks to the Brightray Publishing team, especially Jamie Fleming and Arjan Sudick, for their patient guidance in leading our SalesSparx team through the exhausting but highly rewarding publication journey.

NOTES

1. Some notable business strategy books include:
   - *The Lean Startup: How Today's Entrepreneurs Use Continuous Innovation to Create Radically Successful Businesses* by Eric Ries
   - *Competitive Strategy: Techniques for Analyzing Industries and Competitors* by Michael Porter
   - *Crossing the Chasm: Marketing and Selling High-Tech Products to Mainstream Customers* by Geoffrey Moore
2. Simon Sinek, *Start with Why: How Great Leaders Inspire Everyone to Take Action* (New York: Portfolio, 2011).
3. "AAMC Report Reinforces Mounting Physician Shortage," AAMC, June 11, 2021, https://www.aamc.org/news-insights/press-releases/aamc-report-reinforces-mounting-physician-shortage.
4. Jim Smith and Frank Robinson, "Nail it, then Scale it!" November 23, 2010, http://syncdev.blogspot.com/2010/11/nail-it-then-scale-it.html.
5. Joseph Campbell, *The Hero with a Thousand Faces*, 3rd ed. (Novato, CA: New World Library, 2008).
6. Stephen R. Covey, *The 7 Habits of Highly Effective People: Powerful Lessons in Personal Change* (New York: Free Press, 2004).

7. Jeffrey Pfeffer and Robert I. Sutton, *The Knowing-Doing Gap: How Smart Companies Turn Knowledge into Action* (Cambridge: Harvard Business Review Press, 1999).

INDEX

ABOUT THE AUTHOR

Reese Gomez, founder and CEO of SalesSparx, LCC, is a trusted advisor to software, technology, and services companies that want to accelerate their go-to-market maturity and sales performance. Merging his industrial engineering and performance improvement background with decades of high-growth sales experience, Reese applies a unique perspective to scale sales and revenue predictably.

Before founding SalesSparx, Reese helped to propel several successful healthcare software and service companies to rapid growth. From 2010 to 2012, Reese established and grew a management consulting division from $0 to $60M, and as part of the company's executive leadership, he helped drive overall revenue growth from $50M to $250M. Reese and the SalesSparx team distilled the proven best practices from these experiences and over 10,000 hours of research to create The SalesSparx FUSE, a proven go-to-market and sales acceleration process. Since 2014, SalesSparx has helped more than 100 healthcare solution companies sell more, faster.

Reese has a Bachelor of Science in Industrial Engineering from Stanford University.

FIGURE APPENDIX

Go to www.salessparx.com for high resolution images and other resources.

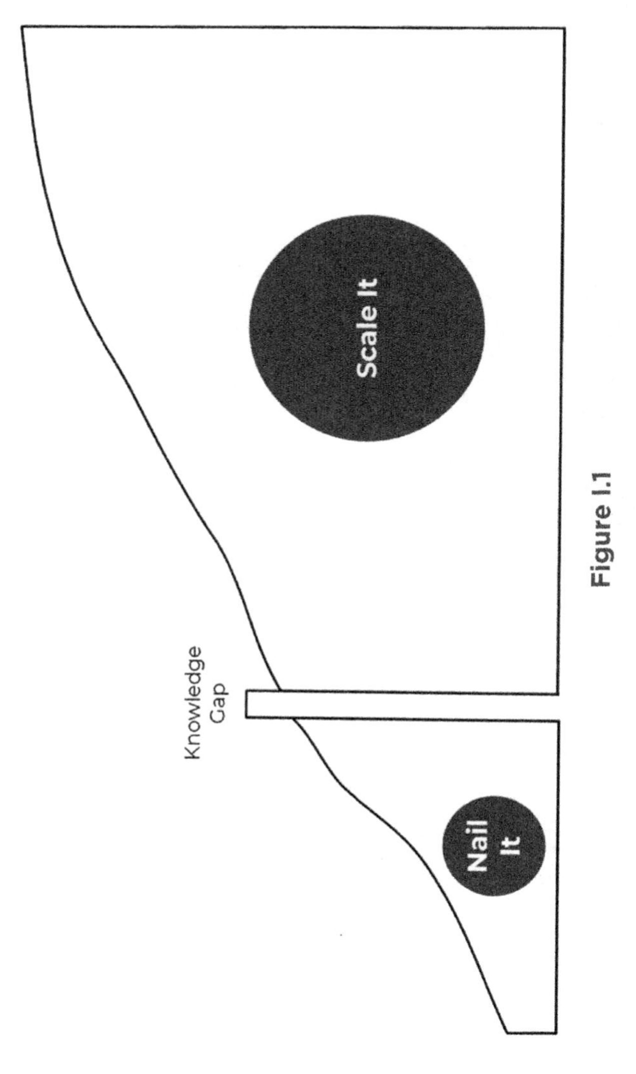

Figure I.1

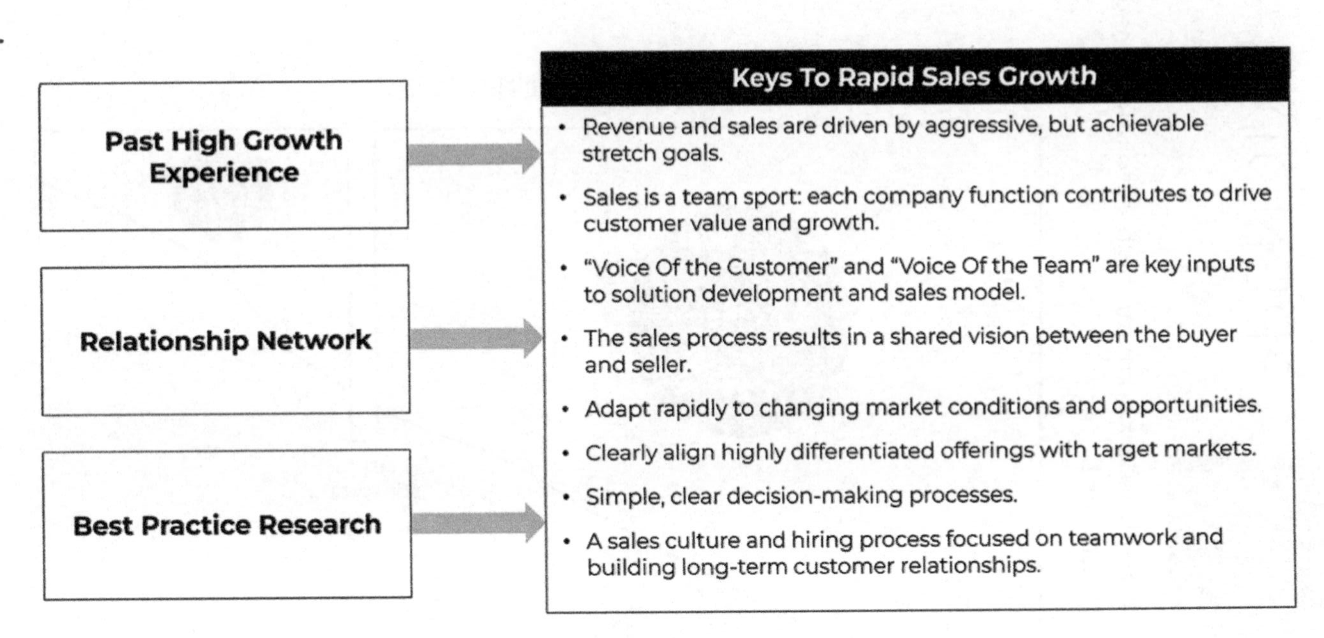
Past High Growth Experience
Relationship Network
Best Practice Research
Keys To Rapid Sales Growth
• Revenue and sales are driven by aggressive, but achievable stretch goals.
• Sales is a team sport: each company function contributes to drive customer value and growth.
• "Voice Of the Customer" and "Voice Of the Team" are key inputs to solution development and sales model.
• The sales process results in a shared vision between the buyer and seller.
• Adapt rapidly to changing market conditions and opportunities.
• Clearly align highly differentiated offerings with target markets.
• Simple, clear decision-making processes.
• A sales culture and hiring process focused on teamwork and building long-term customer relationships.

Figure I.2

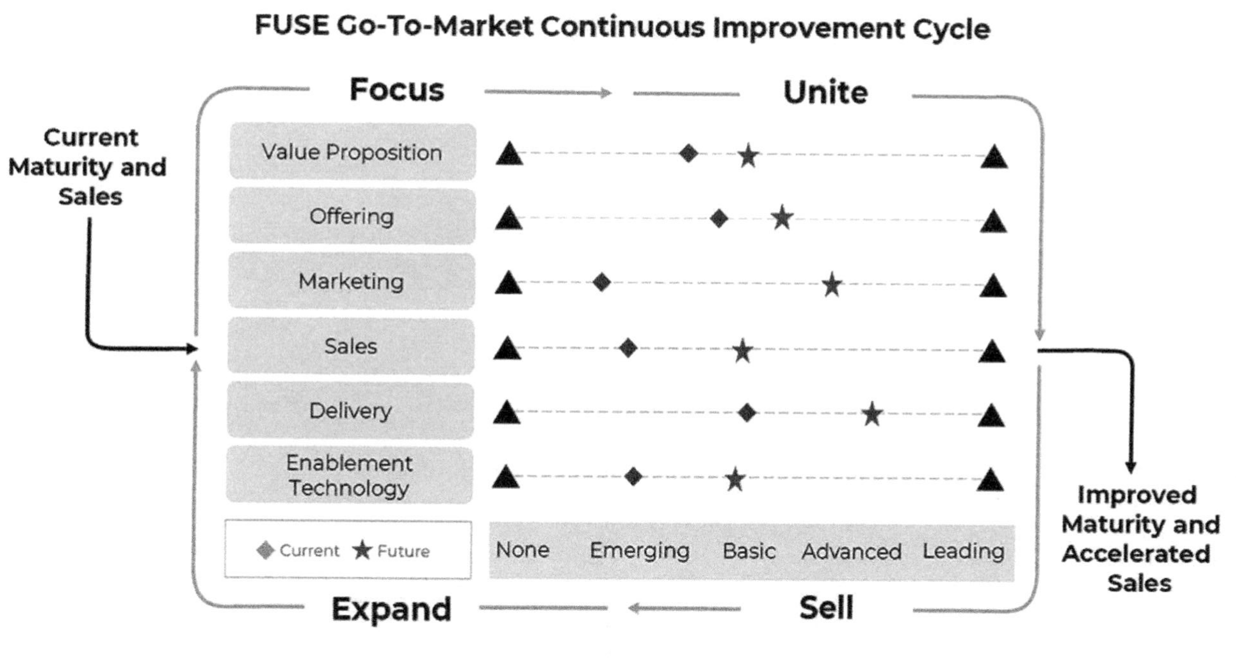
FUSE Go-To-Market Continuous Improvement Cycle
Focus
Unite
Sell
Expand
Current Maturity and Sales
Improved Maturity and Accelerated Sales
Value Proposition
Offering
Marketing
Sales
Delivery
Enablement Technology
Current
Future
None
Emerging
Basic
Advanced
Leading

Figure I.3

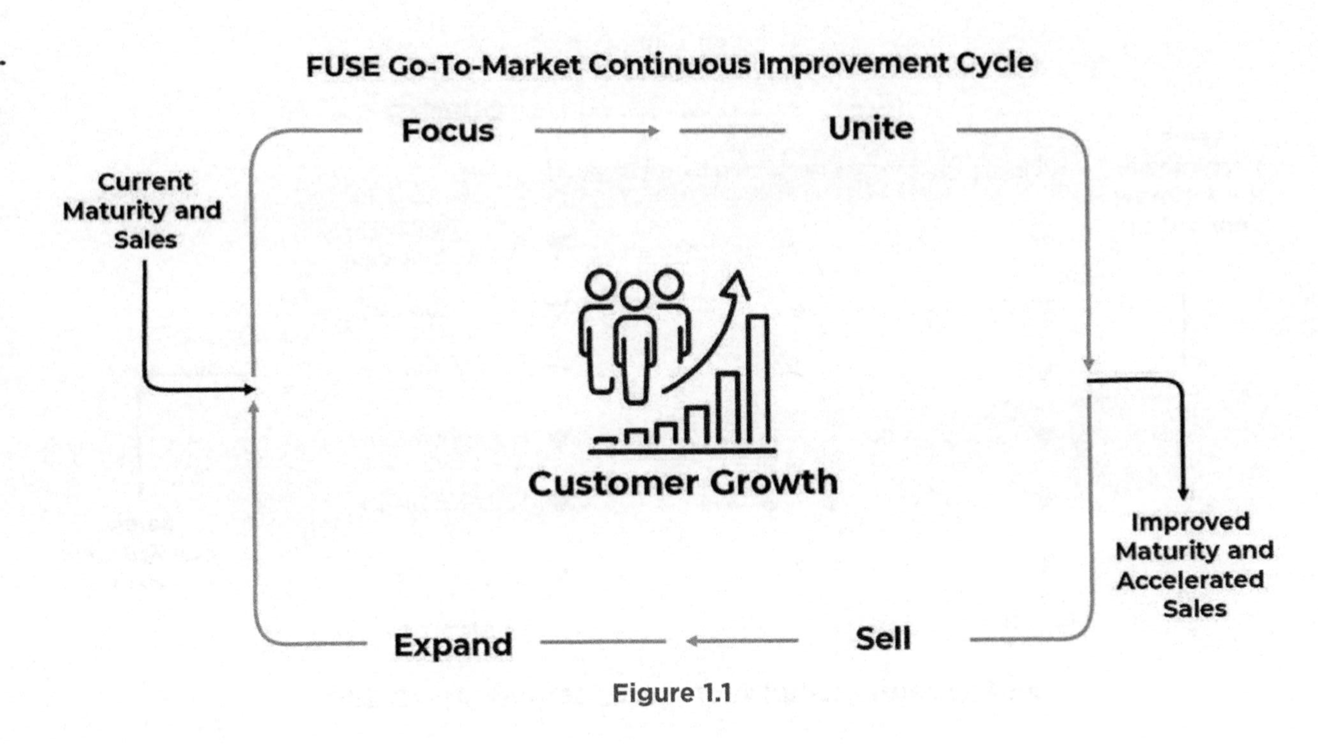
FUSE Go-To-Market Continuous Improvement Cycle
Focus
Unite
Sell
Expand
Current Maturity and Sales
Customer Growth
Improved Maturity and Accelerated Sales

Figure 1.1

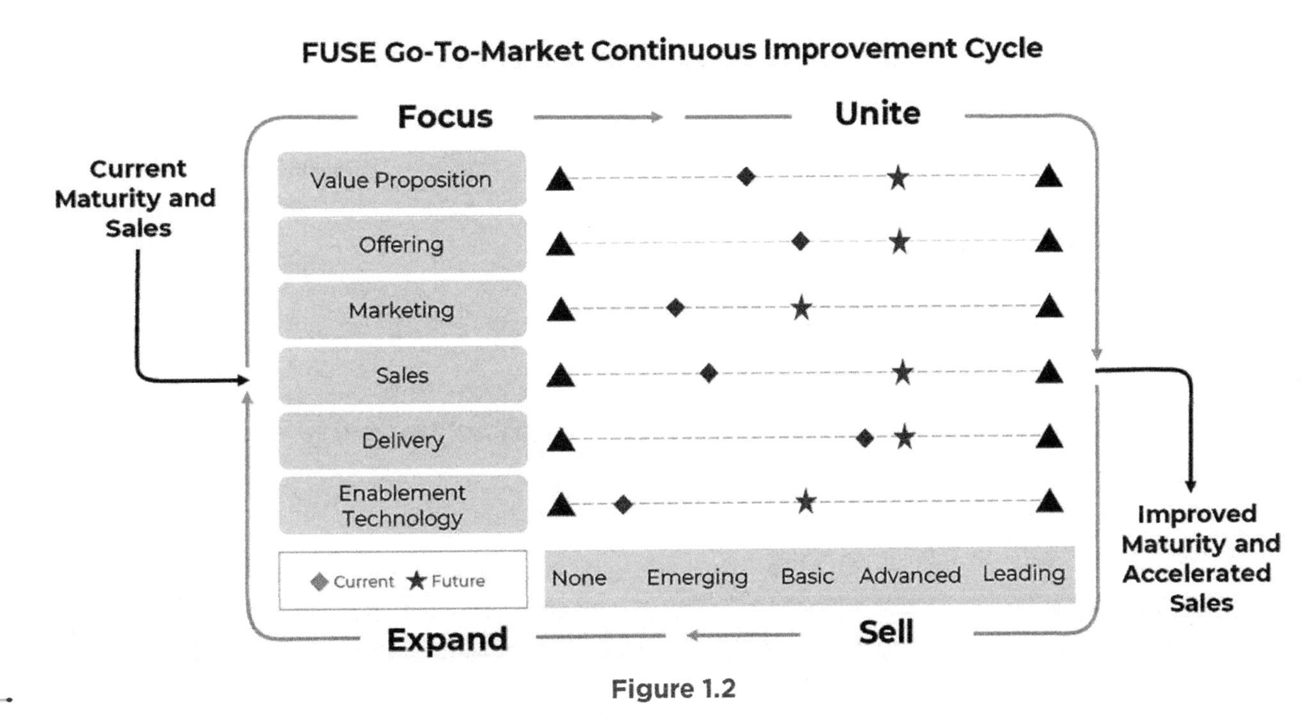
FUSE Go-To-Market Continuous Improvement Cycle
Focus
Unite
Sell
Expand
Current Maturity and Sales
Improved Maturity and Accelerated Sales
Value Proposition
Offering
Marketing
Sales
Delivery
Enablement Technology
Current
Future
None
Emerging
Basic
Advanced
Leading

Figure 1.2

Value Components	Do Nothing	With Solution
Cost/Patient/Year	$1,000	$500
Number of Patients	10,000	10,000
Solution Implementation (Months)	12	6
Total Patient Cost	$10,000,000	$5,000,000
Total Savings	N/A	$5,000,000
Solution Cost	N/A	$1,200,000
Return on Investment		417%

Figure 2.1

Value Components	Do Nothing	With Solution
Cost/Patient/Year	$12,000	$11,500
Number of Patients	50,000	50,000
Solution Implementation (Months)	12	6
Total Patient Cost	$600,000,000	$575,000,000
Total Savings	N/A	$25,000,000
Solution Cost	N/A	$1,200,000
Return on Investment		2083%

Figure 2.2

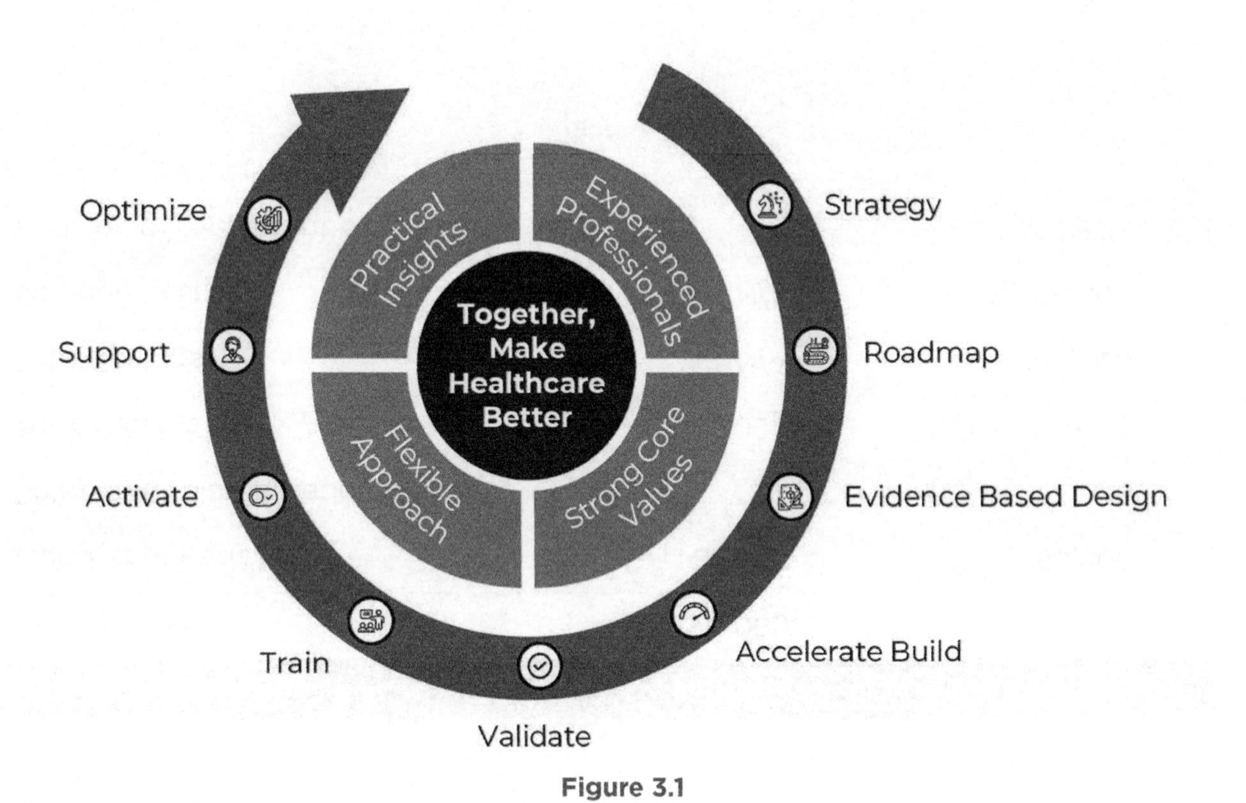
Strategy
Roadmap
Evidence Based Design
Accelerate Build
Validate
Train
Activate
Support
Optimize
Practical Insights
Experienced Professionals
Flexible Approach
Strong Core Values
Together, Make Healthcare Better

Figure 3.1

10% Seller / 90% Buyer

50% Seller / 50% Buyer

90% Seller / 10% Buyer

Teach You

Do It With You

Do It For You

Figure 3.2

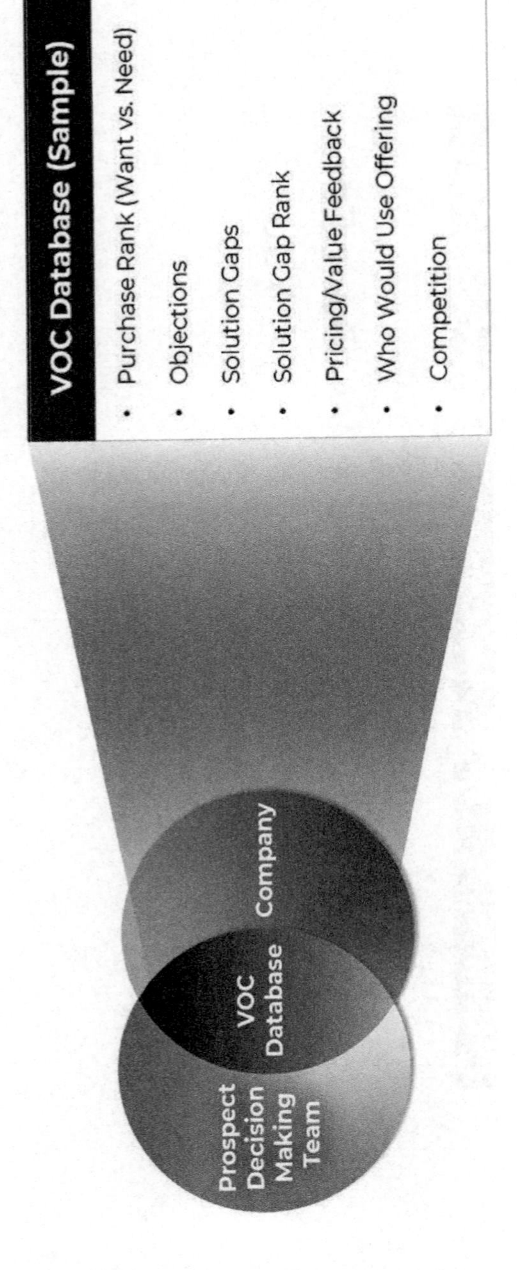

VOC Database (Sample)
• Purchase Rank (Want vs. Need)
• Objections
• Solution Gaps
• Solution Gap Rank
• Pricing/Value Feedback
• Who Would Use Offering
• Competition
Prospect Decision Making Team
VOC Database
Company

Figure 3.3

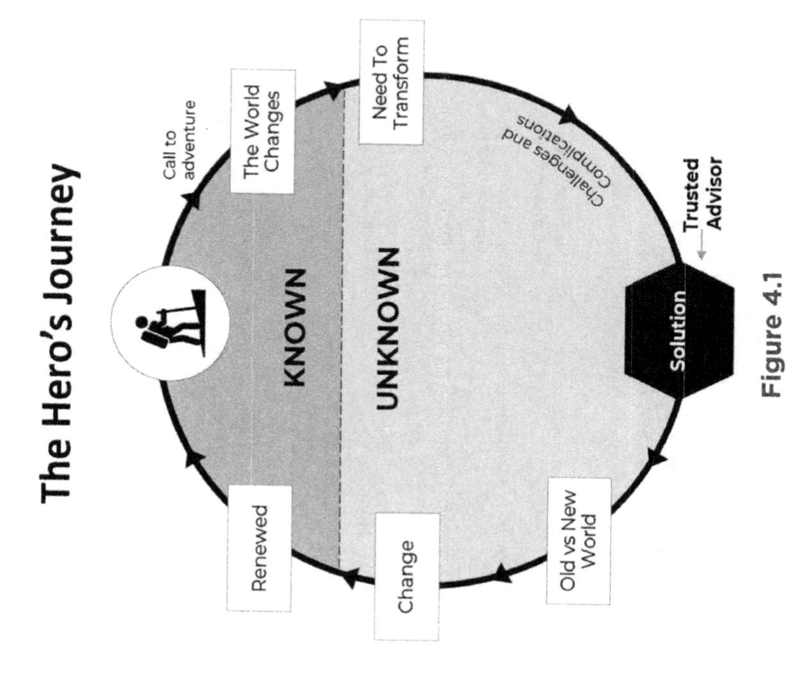
The Hero's Journey
Call to adventure
The World Changes
Need To Transform
Challenges and Complications
Trusted Advisor
Solution
Old vs New World
Change
Renewed
KNOWN
UNKNOWN

Figure 4.1

Buyer Journey - Sample

Buyer Journey	Awareness	Consideration	Decision	Advocacy
Buyer Objectives	• What are others doing? • How do I define the problem? • What are possible solutions?	• What solutions are available? • What is the value of a solution? • What can I learn on my own? • Is this a "need to have" solution? • What will others on the team think? • What is in this for me? • Will it work in our organization? • How can I ensure all stakeholders are aligned? • Is there enough value to justify the solution?	• Can I meet with others that have used the solution? • Help me justify the cost relative to the value. • Have we met all of our decision criteria? • Navigate internal purchasing process. • Have we addressed all regulatory and legal concerns?	• What do I expect? • How will we ensure success? • How will we measure value? • How will we communicate internally and make decisions?

Figure 4.2

Category	No Fit	Workable Fit	Complete Fit	Score
Right Customer	• Full outsourced effective Help Desk solution • Full EHR staff with free time - able to resolve all issues in a timely manner	• Small groups (20-50) with low Help Desk staff • Limited after-hours su pport	• Large independent groups (50-250+) with no staff time • Epic/Allscripts/Cerner • Excessive ticket/call volume	0-15
Right Persona	• Non-Management • Analyst	• VP • Director • Physician	• Application VP • CIO • CIMO • CFO	0-30
Right Pain Points	N/A	• Low staff retention • Future projects gaps • Not enough staff to adequately support providers	• Not meeting current SLAs • High operational cost • No proactive/trending issues analytics • High end user dissatisfaction rates	0-25
Right Triggers	N/A	• Patient/physician satisfaction initiative • Quality of care grade drop	• Upcoming EHR switch • Help Desk RFP	0-30

Figure 4.3

Buyer Journey To SVS Process Map - Sample

Buyer's Journey	Awareness	Consideration			Decision		Advocacy
Buyer Objectives	• What are others doing? • How do I define the problem? • What are possible solutions?	• What solutions are available? • What is the value of a solution? • What can I learn on my own?	• Is this a "need to have" solution? • What will others on the team think? • What is in this for me?	• Will it work in our organization? • How can I ensure all stakeholders are aligned? • Is there enough value to justify the solution?	• Can I meet with others that have used the solution? • Help me justify the cost relative to the value. • Have we met all of our decision criteria?	• Navigate internal purchasing process. • Have we addressed all regulatory and legal concerns?	• What do I expect? • How will we ensure success? • How will we measure value? • How will we communicate internally and make decisions?
Enablement Materials	• Contact Database(s) • Contact Cadence • Case Studies • Customer Testimonials • Interactive Value Calculator • Explainer Videos • Whitepapers	• Lead Scoring (4 Rights Criteria) • Objections and Objection Handling (by persona) • Initial Business Value Calculator (by solution type) • Competitive Battlecards • Intro Presentations • Buyer Journey maps	• Discovery Checklist • Pain Point to Solution Mapping • Ideation Document Template • Business Value Calculator • Maturity Model • SVS Playbook	• Ideation Document Example(s) • Ideation Workshop Agenda • Solution Pricing Model • Insight Stories	• Proposal Template(s) by Solution Type • Contract Template(s)	• Negotiation Strategies • Final Objections and Objection Handling	• Sample Customer Success Criteria • Sample Quarterly Business Reviews
Seller Objectives	• Determine account target (suspect) list based on Ideal Customer Profile • Generate engagement • Generate Marketing Qualified Leads (MQLs) • Generate Outbound Qualified Leads (OQLs)	• Determine "fit" with Qualification Criteria • Select initial insight stories • Develop initial value proposition • Determine single sales objective (opportunity level)	• Develop the Coach • Identified solution priorities • Select Pursuit Team	• Confirm Why Change, Why Now, Why Us? • Define product fit • Develop Ideation Document	• Jointly developed, differentiated vision and solution • Combine buying emotion with compelling business case • Refine Shared Vision	• Develop negotiation strategy and tactics • Win-win business arrangement • Finalize Shared Vision • Contract signature	• Customer success • Develop delivery plan • Execute Shared Vision • Identify add-on business opportunities / account growth
SVS Process	Awareness	Qualification	Discovery	Ideation	Proposal	Negotiate	Partnership

Figure 4.4

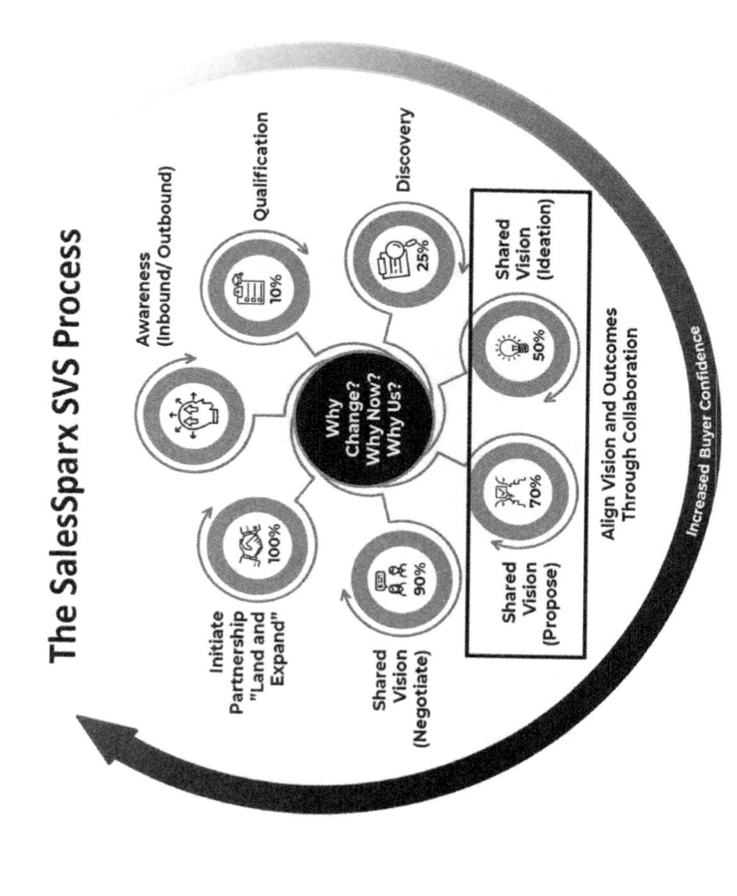

The SalesSparx SVS Process
Why Change? Why Now? Why Us?
Awareness (Inbound/Outbound)
Qualification
10%
Discovery
25%
Shared Vision (Ideation)
50%
70%
Shared Vision (Propose)
Align Vision and Outcomes Through Collaboration
Shared Vision (Negotiate)
90%
Initiate Partnership "Land and Expand"
100%
Increased Buyer Confidence

Figure 5.1

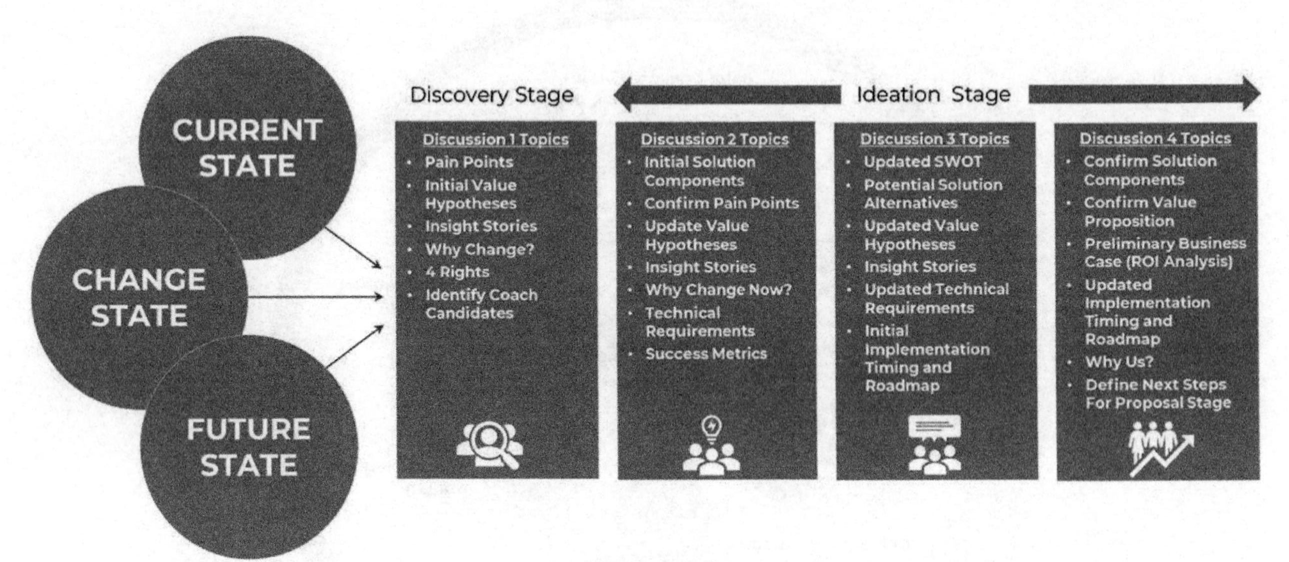
CURRENT STATE
CHANGE STATE
FUTURE STATE
Discovery Stage
Ideation Stage
Discussion 1 Topics
Pain Points
Initial Value Hypotheses
Insight Stories
Why Change?
4 Rights
Identify Coach Candidates
Discussion 2 Topics
Initial Solution Components
Confirm Pain Points
Update Value Hypotheses
Insight Stories
Why Change Now?
Technical Requirements
Success Metrics
Discussion 3 Topics
Updated SWOT
Potential Solution Alternatives
Updated Value Hypotheses
Insight Stories
Updated Technical Requirements
Initial Implementation Timing and Roadmap
Discussion 4 Topics
Confirm Solution Components
Confirm Value Proposition
Preliminary Business Case (ROI Analysis)
Updated Implementation Timing and Roadmap
Why Us?
Define Next Steps For Proposal Stage

Figure 5.2

Seven Habits of Successful Salespeople

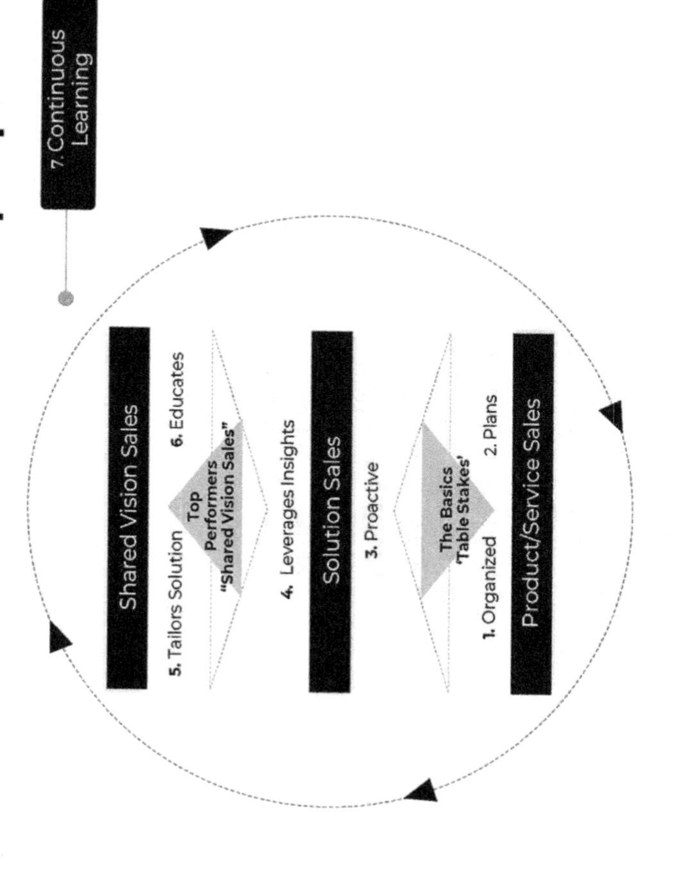

Figure 5.3

Best Practice Sales Process	Improving Sales Conversations	Sales Acceleration Tactics	Sales Productivity	Strategic & Tactical Planning	Healthcare Knowledge
• SVS Overview	• Health Care Executive Conversations	• Buyer Roles	• 7 Habits of Successful Healthcare Salespeople	• Account Planning	• Strategic Priorities
• Market Awareness	• Storytelling	• Finding the Right Coach	• 7 Habits of Successful Sales Managers	• Opportunity Win Planning	• Value-Based Core
• Qualification	• Objection Prevention and Handling	• Handling Red Flags	• Time Management	• Call Planning	• Interoperability
• Discovery	• Collaborative Design Thinking	• Negotiation Tactics		• SWOT Analysis	• Hospital Workflow
• Ideation		• LinkedIn Best Practices		• Prospect Research	• Physician Practice Workflow
• Propose					
• Negotiate					
• Partnership (Land & Expand)					

Figure 5.4

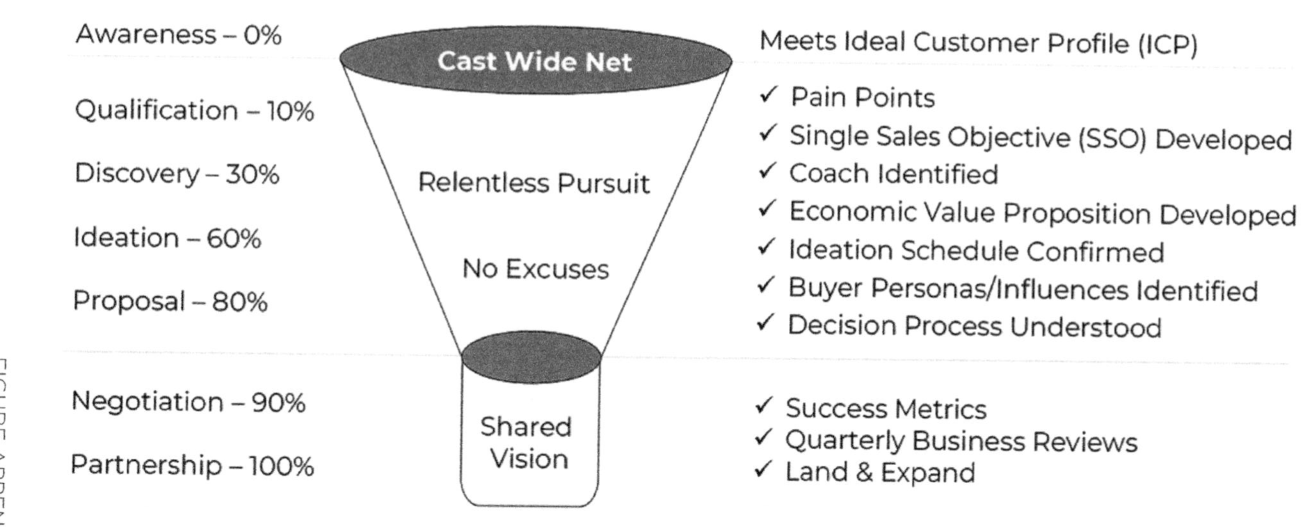

SVS Sales Funnel
Awareness – 0%
Qualification – 10%
Discovery – 30%
Ideation – 60%
Proposal – 80%
Negotiation – 90%
Partnership – 100%
Cast Wide Net
Relentless Pursuit
No Excuses
Shared Vision
Meets Ideal Customer Profile (ICP)
✓ Pain Points
✓ Single Sales Objective (SSO) Developed
✓ Coach Identified
✓ Economic Value Proposition Developed
✓ Ideation Schedule Confirmed
✓ Buyer Personas/Influences Identified
✓ Decision Process Understood
✓ Success Metrics
✓ Quarterly Business Reviews
✓ Land & Expand

Figure 6.1

Revenue Machine Report - Sample

Sales Process	Unique Web Visits/ Month	MQLs* /Visits	MQLs/ Month	SQL/ MQL	Web Based SQLs/ Month	Decision-Maker Meetings / Month	SQL/ Meetings	SQLs/ Year	Win Rate	Wins	Average Deal Size (ARR)	Contracted ARR
Current Revenue Machine	100	0	0	0	0	8	5%	48	35%	17	$350,000	~$6M
With SalesSparx FUSE	2,000	1%	20	10%	2	100	10%	96	35%	34	$400,000	$13.6M
With SalesSparx FUSE (Stretch)*	**5,000**	**2%**	**100**	**20%**	**20**	**100**	**15%**	**168**	**40%**	**67**	**$500,000**	**$33.5M**

*MQL – Marketing Qualified Lead, SQL – Sales Qualified Lead, ARR – Annualized Recurring Revenue

Figure 6.2

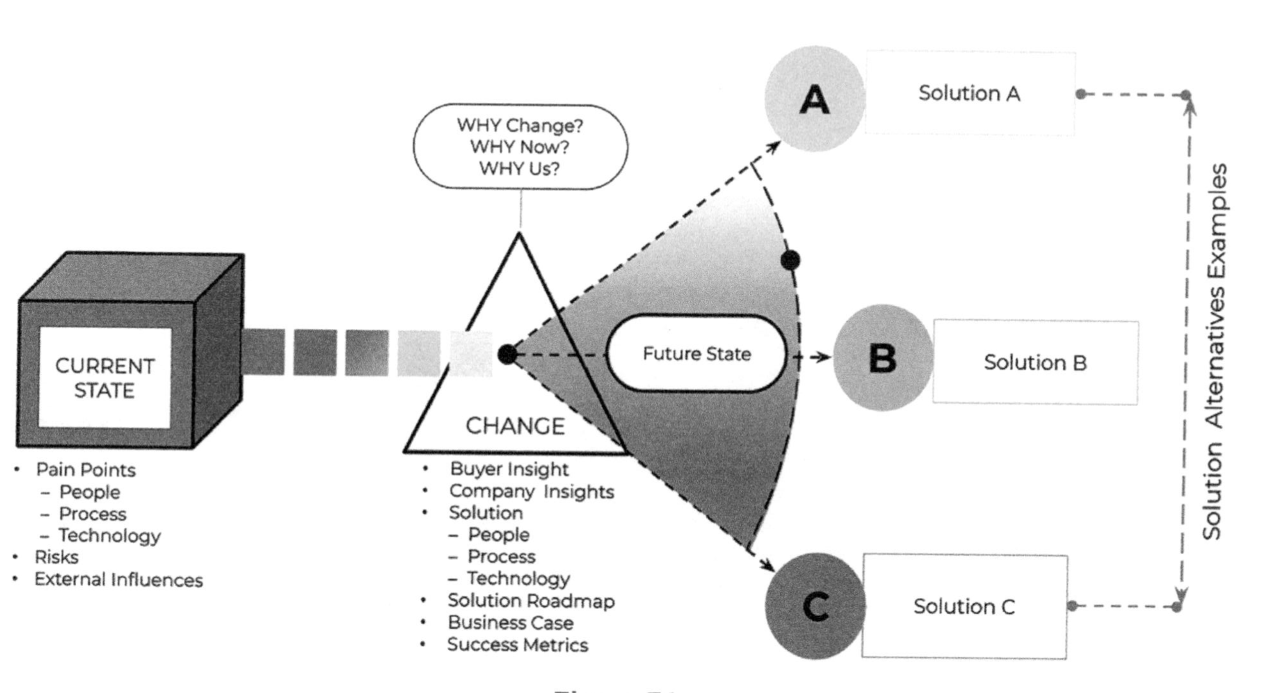
CURRENT STATE
• Pain Points
– People
– Process
– Technology
• Risks
• External Influences
WHY Change?
WHY Now?
WHY Us?
CHANGE
• Buyer Insight
• Company Insights
• Solution
– People
– Process
– Technology
• Solution Roadmap
• Business Case
• Success Metrics
Future State
A
B
C
Solution A
Solution B
Solution C
Solution Alternatives Examples

Figure 7.1

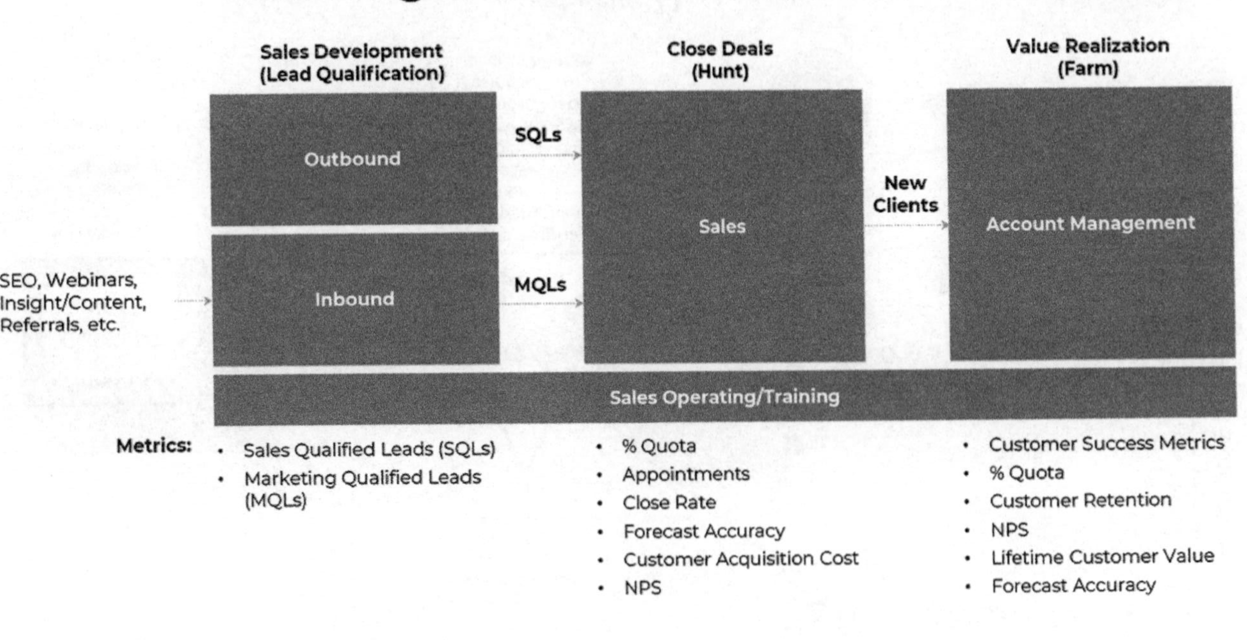
Sales Organization Process/Metrics - Sample
Sales Development
(Lead Qualification)
Close Deals
(Hunt)
Value Realization
(Farm)
Outbound
Inbound
SQLs
MQLs
Sales
New
Clients
Account Management
SEO, Webinars,
Insight/Content,
Referrals, etc.
Sales Operating/Training
Metrics:
• Sales Qualified Leads (SQLs)
• Marketing Qualified Leads (MQLs)
• % Quota
• Appointments
• Close Rate
• Forecast Accuracy
• Customer Acquisition Cost
• NPS
• Customer Success Metrics
• % Quota
• Customer Retention
• NPS
• Lifetime Customer Value
• Forecast Accuracy

Figure 7.2

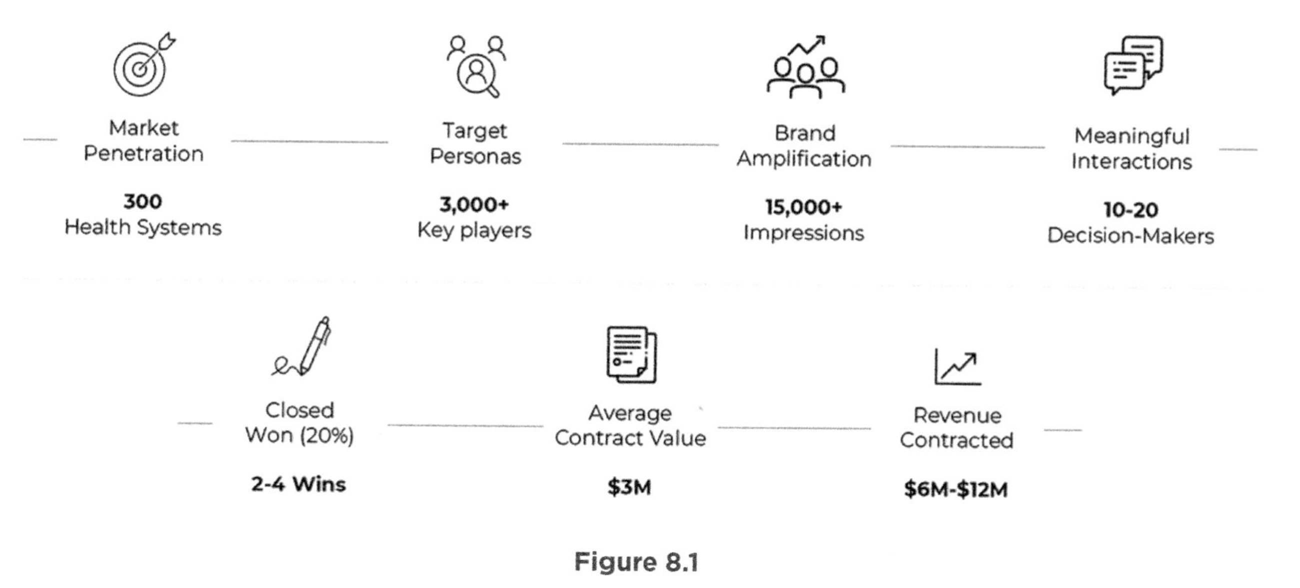
Market Penetration
300
Health Systems
Target Personas
3,000+
Key players
Brand Amplification
15,000+
Impressions
Meaningful Interactions
10-20
Decision-Makers
Closed Won (20%)
2-4 Wins
Average Contract Value
$3M
Revenue Contracted
$6M-$12M

Figure 8.1

Printed in Great Britain
by Amazon